Athletes of Purpose

50 People Who Changed the Face of Sports

Arnold B. Cheyney
Emeritus Professor
University of Miami

Good Year Books
An Imprint of Pearson Learning

DEDICATION

To the memory of Coach Junius B. Ferrall 1911–1995

ACKNOWLEDGEMENTS

Most athletes, however gifted or average, have at least one coach that made a significant difference in their lives and added many memories. My personal memory, among many, is of the half-time pep talks of my football coach. Coach Junius B. Ferrall's admonitions ran something like this: "Play your best, for you will replay these games in your minds the rest of your lives." Sure, Coach, you bet!

Now in my seventies, I am startled from time to time because I still replay those 1940s games in my mind. I say to myself, "If I had only. . . ." Coach Ferrall made a difference in my life and in the lives of countless others.

Athletes of Purpose gave me great joy in its writing. Much of the credit for that joy goes to the children's department of the Wooster Public Library. The staff helped me time and again with my search for background material. Denise Cheyney, my daughter-in-law, was very helpful with her knowledge of the Internet, as was my wife, Jeanne, who once again spent much time proofing the many drafts of the manuscript. Any shortcomings herein are attributable to the author.

Photo Credits

Unless otherwise acknowledged, all photos are the property of Scott, Foresman and Company.
Page abbreviations are as follows: (T) top, (C) center, (B) bottom, (L) left, and (R) right.
Front cover: (TL) SportsChrome, (BL) Reuters/Corbis-Bettmann, (C) Andy Hayt/DUOMO,
(TR) Corbis-Bettmann, (BR) Reuters/Corbis-Bettmann; Back cover: (L) UPI/Corbis-Bettmann, (R) Chris Trotman/DUOMO.
2 AP/Wide World; 4 DUOMO; 6 Mitch Gerber/Corbis; 8 Rich Kane/SportsChrome East/West;
10 UPI/Corbis-Bettmann; 12 Steve Raymer/Corbis; 14 William R. Sallaz/DUOMO; 16 SportsChrome East/West;
18 UPI/Corbis-Bettmann; 20 UPI/Corbis-Bettmann; 22 UPI/Corbis-Bettmann; 24 UPI/Corbis-Bettmann;
26 Laurie Warner/SportsChrome East/West; 28 UPI/Corbis-Bettmann; 30 AP/Wide World; 32 Reuters/Corbis-Bettmann;
34 Reuters/Corbis-Bettmann; 36 Paul J. Sutton/DUOMO; 38 UPI/Corbis-Bettmann; 40 UPI/Corbis-Bettmann;
42 UPI/Corbis-Bettmann; 44 Rich Kane/SportsChrome East/West; 46 UPI/Corbis-Bettmann; 48 DUOMO;
50 UPI/Corbis-Bettmann; 52 Steven Sutton/DUOMO; 54 DUOMO; 56 SportsChrome East/West; 58 UPI/Corbis-Bettmann;
60 Chris Trotman/DUOMO; 62 AP/Wide World; 64 UPI/Corbis-Bettmann; 66 UPI/Corbis-Bettmann; 68 UPI/Corbis-Bettmann;
70 Reuters/Corbis-Bettmann; 72 UPI/Corbis-Bettmann; 74 AP/Wide World; 76 UPI/Corbis-Bettmann;
78 Steven E. Sutton/DUOMO; 80 DUOMO; 82 DUOMO; 84 AP/Wide World; 86 AP/Wide World; 88 UPI/Corbis-Bettmann;
90 UPI/Corbis-Bettmann; 92 AP/Wide World; 94 UPI/Corbis-Bettmann; 96 Corbis-Bettmann; 98 Reuters/Corbis-Bettmann;
100 UPI/Corbis-Bettmann.

Silhouettes

All silhouettes are taken from Image Bank DigitArt Clip Art Volumes 19 and 25, Eyewire Studios.

A GOOD YEAR BOOK®

Good Year Books
are available for most basic curriculum subjects plus many enrichment areas. For more Good Year Books, contact your local bookseller or educational dealer. For a complete catalog with information about other Good Year Books, please write:

Good Year Books
Pearson Learning
299 Jefferson
Parsippany, NJ 07054
Book design by Foster Design.

Printed in the United States of America.
0-673-58667-7

1 2 3 4 5 6 7 8 9 — ML — 07 06 05 04 03 02 01 00 99

Preface

The athletes in this volume have two personality traits in common: they set goals and made the sacrifices necessary to attain them. The primary sacrifice was hours of tedious practice. All of us, child or adult, need to be reminded that real success comes through sacrifice.

Juvenile books about these athletes are generally available in libraries, even though they may be out of print. Some of the athletes are included in special volumes along with other players. The athletes were chosen based on the character they displayed while playing the sport or sports in which they excelled. Also, I considered it important to feature a variety of sports so children realize that some sports are lifetime activities and not just for the years of youth with its attendant vigor.

My most agonizing moments involved making choices as to who would make the final cut, to apply a sport term to a literary predicament. I can only suggest that parents and teachers go with their children to the library or bookstore, perhaps the Internet, and find a biography of a sport hero or heroine not found in these pages. Then read together.

Athletes of Purpose is intended as a link to further reading and study; the biographies are short by intention so as to fulfill this connection. The Further Reading lists are exactly that. The books listed are presently in libraries somewhere, along with many others of the same sort. Some books about these athletes are now in the process of being published. They may be found in your local library, through interlibrary loan, or in bookstores.

Parents and teachers are encouraged to read the biographies aloud to children or a group of children. The questions and activities are designed to deepen the thought processes of those who have listened or read the material. Think of the Further Reading list as an assignment.

The pages are perforated on the inside edges for separating and copying. They can then be used with individuals and small groups. The limitation on their use in this form is determined by the creativity of the instructor. The Index on page 105 lists the sports in which these athletes participated and their relationships with other athletes.

Specific Ways to Use This Book

1. Reserve class time to share thoughts generated by the biography or the reading list in the Further Reading section.

2. Encourage children to keep a log of what they read. Set time aside so they may share what they wrote in their logs.

3. Encourage children to read aloud the *Athletes of Purpose* biographies with younger or older persons, especially senior citizens.

4. Read paragraphs from the biographies that make a person feel good. Share them with each other in small groups.

5. Read the sentence thought to be most quotable. Memorize the quote and share it at the dinner table at home. Discuss the family's reaction the following day with classmates.

6. Select the biography most enjoyed. Dress in the uniform of the athlete and read the biography in front of the class or in an assembly.

7. Create a class mural of a specific sport and emphasize the athletes found in these pages.

8. Read portions of a biography that make one feel uneasy. Explain the reasons for these feelings, if possible.

9. Using girl and boy dolls, create uniforms for sports figures in *Athletes of Purpose.*

10. Retell an *Athletes of Purpose* biography using flannelboard characters.

11. Read parts that prove a point or a certain point of view.

12. Create and deliver a twenty-word telegram to another person in class urging him or her to read about a specific athlete.

13. Create a comic strip of one of the athletes in *Athletes of Purpose.* (Study some comic strips from a Sunday newspaper first.)

14. Have an "Athlete of the Day Read-a-Thon." During the day, encourage children to read in small groups about their favorite athletes.

15. Create book jackets for specific sports. Have the children include their own illustrations, the records and awards of the athletes, and the athletes' public service contributions. Show the stapled sports books at a Back to School Night, PTA, or PTO meeting.

16. Read parts aloud from *Athletes of Purpose* that have the element of surprise.

17. Create a dance using movements that athletes make during games or Olympic competitions. Do the dance before a group and see how many in the audience can recognize the sports that are illustrated by the movements.

18. Create a portfolio titled "Celebration of an Athlete." Include in the portfolio copies of the biographies from *Athletes of Purpose,* photos of the athletes from newspapers or sports cards, newspaper clippings, student illustrations and writing, records and awards, and Internet information. Encourage the students to make a Table of Contents for their portfolio in chronological order or another logical arrangement.

19. Jot down ideas and questions as you read. What else would you like to know about these athletes? Use the Further Reading lists as a starting point to find answers to questions.

20. Set a period at the end of the week to discuss one specific athlete on which the students agree. Have each student read about that person. Order a video or film about the athlete from the school audiovisual department or the children's department of your public library. Discuss the film in light of what was learned from books and other materials.

21. For those with access to the Internet, search for athletes who are still living and find what they are now doing. Report findings to the class.

22. Create a mural titled "Classroom Wall of Athletic Fame" highlighting students' favorite athletes. Later, honor others who led purposeful lives: people from scientific, medical, political, religious, or other professions.

23. Set aside time during the day for "Reading and Writing Together About My Favorite Athlete." Reserve the last fifteen minutes for writing about the athlete. You, the teacher, should also participate in this exercise by reading and writing, too.

Contents

Athletes of Purpose

Henry "Hank" Aaron

1934 • Baseball

Herbert and Estella Aaron had eight children during the Great Depression. The family lived in Mobile, Alabama, among other poor black families. Henry was their third child. Their home had no windows or lights, but they did have a kerosene lamp, love, and space around them—space to play ball.

Baseball was Henry's favorite sport. He gathered bottle caps and hit them with a broomstick. Caps that went the farthest he called home runs; shorter ones he called singles and doubles. He wrapped nylon stockings or cloth around old golf balls and bound them tightly together to make baseballs. Henry then tossed them on the roof of the house and caught them as they tumbled down. For a change, he tossed them over the roof, ran around to the other side, and caught them before they hit the ground.

Henry stopped playing high school football for fear he might hurt himself and ruin a baseball career. In high school, he learned that Jackie Robinson, an African American man, had broken the color barrier and was playing for the Brooklyn Dodgers in the all-white major leagues. Henry skipped school in the afternoons and listened to the radio at the pool hall as the announcer described Jackie's playing.

When the high school principal found out about Henry's absences, he expelled him. Henry did not tell his parents, but he did go to school. He just walked in the front door and out the back and went on to the pool hall. Shortly thereafter, his father stood in the pool hall entrance looking at him. After a long talk about the necessity of a high school education, Henry went back to school.

A baseball scout heard about Henry and his baseball talent. He signed Henry with the Indianapolis Clowns of the Negro American League. Soon the 18-year-old was batting fourth in the Clowns' lineup, playing shortstop and hitting over .400. Henry's practice in hitting floating bottle caps and racing around the house to catch his "baseball" was paying off. The Clowns won the Negro League World Series, and Henry was still able to graduate from high school, to the delight of his mother and father.

Henry joined the Milwaukee Braves and was given the nickname "Hank." In 1954 the Braves called him to their spring training camp. One of the regular players had fractured an ankle sliding into second base. The next day, Hank Aaron was playing left field for the major league team. In April he hit his first big league home run.

Becoming a major league player in the 1950s was not easy. Hank was subjected to racial slurs and anonymous death threats. He countered this cowardice by his dignified manner and excellent playing. As he got older, he married and started a family, and his accomplishments on the baseball field grew. By the time he retired from baseball after the 1976 season, he had hit more home runs in his career than any other player in the history of the game.

Reading

1. In your estimation, who are the best major league baseball players in the game today? What makes each one great? Share your choices with your classmates.
2. What is your favorite sport? What nickname would you choose for yourself in that sport? Why?
3. Major league baseball records are constantly being made and broken. What are some recent ones that are important to fans and players?
4. Write a title for the biography of Hank Aaron. Compare your title with those of your classmates.

Social Studies

1. Hank Aaron was elected to the National Baseball Hall of Fame in 1982. Where is it located?
2. Hank Aaron had a record 755 home runs during his career. Whose record did he break?
3. What baseball stadium is the closest to your home? What is the name of the home team that plays there?
4. Prepare a report on Little League Baseball for your classmates. Where is its headquarters?

Further Reading

Deane, Bill. *Top 10 Baseball Hitters*. Springfield, NJ: Enslow Publishers, 1998.

_________. *Top 10 Baseball Home Run Hitters*. Springfield, NJ: Enslow Publishers, 1997.

The Lincoln Library of Sports Champions. Volume 16. Columbus, OH: Frontier Press Company, 1993.

Margolies, Jacob. *Hank Aaron: Home Run King*. New York: Franklin Watts, 1992.

Rennert, Richard Scott. *Henry Aaron: Baseball Great*. New York: Chelsea House Publishers, 1993.

Sullivan, George. *Sluggers: Twenty-Seven of Baseball's Greatest*. New York: Atheneum, 1991.

Tackach, James. *Hank Aaron*. New York: Chelsea House Publishers, 1992.

Kareem Abdul-Jabbar | 1947 • Basketball

At birth, Ferdinand Lewis Alcindor, Jr., weighed 13 pounds and was 22½ inches long. As a pro basketball player, he was 260 pounds and 7 feet 2 inches tall.

In the elementary grades, Lew was awkward and uncoordinated, but he exercised and practiced and soon was able to hold his own on the basketball court. In the seventh grade, he was given the number 33 to wear, never realizing, at the time, that he would be wearing it throughout his career. In the eighth grade, he made his first "dunk," jumping high and putting the basketball down through the hoop.

For his high school education, he chose to go to a private Catholic school, Power Memorial in New York City. In his 3 years there, the team lost only one game and had a 71-game winning streak! He finished high school with 2,067 points. Naturally, many colleges wanted him to attend their schools. Lew chose UCLA, the University of California at Los Angeles, where Coach John Wooden stressed the importance of grades as well as basketball. At that time, freshmen in college could not play on the varsity squads in regular-season play. UCLA's varsity had recently won the national basketball championship. In the fall of 1965, a game was organized in which the freshmen would play against the varsity in UCLA's new 12,500-seat arena. The freshmen beat the varsity players 75 to 60! Lew made 31 points.

For the 3 years Lew played varsity basketball at UCLA, the team won three national championships. Overall, they won eighty-eight games and lost only two. During this period, Lew took instruction in the Muslim faith. He graduated with a degree in history from UCLA and later officially changed his name from Lew Alcindor to Kareem Abdul-Jabbar, "the powerful servant of Allah."

Of course, teams in the professional basketball leagues wanted him to play center for them. He decided that each one should make its best offer. Kareem would take the best of those. He signed with Milwaukee even though the other team offered to give him much more money than it had originally planned. He proved, however, to be a man of his word.

Kareem was voted the league's Most Valuable Player several times. The Los Angeles Lakers offered him a lifetime contract. Back in southern California, he not only played basketball, but he married and had four children. Another career, television, opened up for him. In 1979 "Magic" Johnson joined the team and the Lakers began winning even more games.

The 1988-89 season would be his last. He had played professional basketball for a record 20 years, and he was the oldest player in the National Basketball Association. Kareem ended his career with 38,387 points, and the Lakers retired his jersey, number 33.

Reading

1. After reading Kareem's biography, make up a title that best expresses what you think of him.
2. Draw a picture of Kareem playing basketball as a professional. Add a caption below your picture explaining what he is doing.
3. After reading one or two other biographies about Kareem, list three positive character traits that you find in his life story. Compare your list with those of your classmates.
4. Kareem studied and then embraced the Muslim faith. What distinctive beliefs do you have? List some of them.

Social Studies

1. Kareem remarked that even though a basketball player can make a basket from 25 feet, it does not make him the kind of person who can tell you how to live your life. What does this statement mean to you?
2. In a reference book, read about Los Angeles, California. Make a list of five places that would interest you if you could visit the area. Discuss your list with your classmates.
3. As a student at UCLA, Kareem majored in history. At this time in your life, what do you think will be your major in college? In twenty-five words or less, write why you would choose that major area of study. Discuss it with your parents and classmates.

Further Reading

Anderson, Dave. *The Story of Basketball.* New York: William Morrow and Company, 1988.

Borello, Helen. *Kareem Abdul-Jabbar*. New York: Chelsea House Publishers, 1995.

Coburn, R. Thomas. *Kareem Abdul-Jabbar: Basketball Great*. New York: Chelsea House Publishers, 1995.

Dunnahoo, Terry Janson and Herma Silverstein. *Basketball Hall of Fame.* New York: Crestwood House, 1994.

Knapp, Ron. *Top 10 Basketball Scorers.* Hillside, NJ: Enslow Publishers, 1994.

The Lincoln Library of Sports Champions. Volume 1. Columbus, OH: Frontier Press Company, 1993.

Margolies, Jacob. *Kareem Abdul-Jabbar: Basketball Great*. New York: Franklin Watts, 1992.

Miller, Faye Young and Wayne Coffey. *Winning Basketball for Girls.* New York: Facts on File, 1992.

Sanford, William R. and Carl R. Green. *Kareem Abdul-Jabbar.* New York: Crestwood House, 1993.

Sehnert, Chris W. *Top 10 Big Men*. Edina, MN: Abdo & Daughters, 1997.

Sullivan, George. *Center.* New York: Thomas Y. Crowell, 1988.

Twelve-year-old Cassius Clay and his best friend were riding their bicycles in Louisville, Kentucky. Cassius's father had just bought his son a new Schwinn bike. To get out of the rain, the two boys went to the Home Show, where there was free popcorn and hot dogs. When Cassius returned for his bicycle, it was gone. Someone told him to see the off-duty policeman, Joe Martin, at a nearby gym. While Cassius told Joe his story, he was actually watching the boys who were sparring, shadow boxing, and jumping rope in the gym. He would soon know what he wanted to do with his life: box.

Cassius's parents, desiring to keep him out of a gang, signed a parental consent form and Cassius began to learn the art of boxing. Early in the mornings, he ran for miles and skipped rope. During the day, he went to school. After school he cleaned rooms at a nearby college. Then he went to Joe's gym for a couple of hours. Later in the evening, he worked in another gym on timing, rhythm, and counter-punching. By the age of 16, he was 6 feet tall, weighed 170 pounds, and was still growing.

In 1960 he won the Amateur Athletic Union (AAU) title, which qualified him for the Olympic Trials. After winning the Trials, he went to Rome, Italy, for the Summer Olympics, proclaiming, "I am the greatest!" He backed up his boast, winning a gold medal. On returning to Louisville, Kentucky, he received a hero's welcome. But because he was black, he could not be served a hamburger and milk shake in a restaurant at that time. In the same restaurant, a motorcycle gang, wearing Nazi symbols on their black jackets, could be served. Cassius threw his gold medal into the river.

After the Olympics, Cassius turned professional, and in 1964 he won the heavyweight title from Sonny Liston. After the fight, he announced his conversion to the religion of the Nation of Islam and changed his name to Muhammad Ali. Becoming a Black Muslim brought Ali a great deal of criticism from white and black people alike. But he countered with "I'm free to be who I want."

Ali's rematch with Liston lasted one minute and fifty-two seconds. He went on to beat many other heavyweight fighters, but his biggest fight was against the United States government. Ali refused to join the U.S. military because he was now a Muslim minister and opposed to war. Ali was banned from boxing, convicted for draft evasion, and stripped of his heavyweight title. After 4 years of costly legal battles, the Supreme Court ruled unanimously in Ali's favor.

Ali came back to win his heavyweight title again, only to lose it and win it once more. He fought in many countries and had a vast following of fans all over the world. A slurring of his speech and other symptoms were diagnosed as Parkinson's Disease, which had been caused by repeated blows to his head. Now Ali enjoys spending time with his wife and eight children, does charitable work in developing countries, and is remembered by many fans as "The Greatest."

Reading

1. Who would be the best audience for the biography of Muhammad Ali? Practice reading it aloud and then read it to someone you think would find it interesting.
2. Do any of the incidents in the life of Muhammad Ali bring back memories of something that happened to you? Explain the situations to your classmates, if you feel comfortable in doing so.
3. Ali enjoyed creating poetry. He wrote about a fight he was to have with Sonny Liston: "If you like to lose money/Be a fool and bet on Sonny." Write a short poem about Ali and share it with your classmates.
4. In your library, check out one of the books from the Further Reading list about Ali. Report on several items that interest you and that were not mentioned in the *Athletes of Purpose* biography.

Social Studies

1. Muhammad Ali boxed in many cities of the world: Vancouver, Canada; Djakarta, Indonesia; Dublin, Ireland; Rome, Italy; Tokyo, Japan; Manila, Philippines; Zurich, Switzerland; and Kinshasa, Zaire (now Congo). Find the countries and cities on a map or globe.
2. Those who refused to fight in the war in Vietnam were labeled "conscientious objectors." Look up this term in a reference book. Then make a list of reasons why someone might refuse to participate in a war.
3. In a reference book, search for information about Parkinson's Disease. Discuss what you learned with your classmates.
4. Many people have been treated unfairly in the past, as was Muhammad Ali. Think of a time when you were treated unfairly. How did you cope with the situation? If you had to do it over, would you react differently? How?

Further Reading

Conklin. Thomas. *Muhammad Ali: The Fight for Respect.* Brookfield, CT: The Millbrook Press, 1991.

Denenberg, Barry. *The Story of Muhammad: Heavyweight Champion of the World.* New York: Dell Publishing, 1990.

Fitzgerald, Jim. *Boxing for Beginners.* New York: Atheneum, 1980.

Knapp, Ron. *Top 10 Heavyweight Boxers.* Springfield, NJ: Enslow Publishers, 1997.

The Lincoln Library of Sports Champions. Volume 1. Columbus, OH: Frontier Press Company, 1993.

Ricciuti, Edward R. *How to Box: A Guide for Beginners.* New York: Thomas Y. Crowell, 1982.

Rummel, Jack. *Muhammad Ali.* New York: Chelsea House Publications, 1988.

Sanford, William R. and Carl R. Green. *Muhammad Ali.* New York: Crestwood House, 1993.

Sullivan, George. *Great Lives: Sports.* New York: Charles Scribner's Sons, 1988.

Mario Andretti

Mario Andretti was born five hours before his twin brother, Aldo. The small Italian town in which they grew up was on the peninsula of Istria, south of Trieste. Their father, "Gigi," owned seven farms, so they were prosperous. With their mother, Rina, and older sister, Anna Maria, they were a happy family.

At the end of World War II, Italy and its allies, known as the Axis powers, lost the war. In the settlement ending the war, the Istrian peninsula became part of Yugoslavia, and a communist state. To retain their Italian citizenship, they were given the opportunity to move into Italy. For 7 years Mario and his family lived at Lucca, about 45 miles from Florence. They had one room and shared a bathroom with other families.

The two boys were thrilled when their uncle let them drive his motorcycle. He even built them a wooden car to race down hills. When they were 13, Aldo talked an owner of a garage into letting them park cars. Aldo failed to mention that they had never driven an automobile before! They learned quickly and automobiles became their life.

About this time, a racing organization was formed for Italian youngsters aged 14 to 21. Its purpose was to prepare them for Italian car racing when they were older. Even though they were only thirteen, the two boys managed to get into the program. The garage owner had a small car they could drive. The big hurdle was their father. He was totally against race car driving for his boys. But the brothers kept their car racing a secret.

Then their great plans were turned upside down, for the family had an opportunity to move to the United States in 1955. Mario's uncle sponsored them, for he had lived in the United States since 1909. When they got to their new home in Nazareth, Pennsylvania, they found a race track. Since they had no car, they decided to rebuild one from scratch: a 1948 Hudson Hornet.

Soon the two boys were winning races. Then Aldo crashed and was in a coma for 2 weeks. They could not hide this from their father. He would not speak to them for 6 months. But he did let them live at home. In 1961 Mario married Dee Ann Hoch. She encouraged him to make race car driving a career.

Mario raced every kind of vehicle he could, from motorcycles, midget cars, stock cars, and dirt cars to the finest custom-made race cars in the Indianapolis 500 races. He was injured several times: broken ribs, a cracked pelvis, a broken clavicle, and multiple burns on his hands and face. Even so, Mario missed only two races because of injury.

Mario Andretti won the Indianapolis 500, the Daytona 500, and the Formula One Grand Prix; he was the first race car driver to do so. He is also the only person to win the Driver of the Year Award in three different decades. Mario retired from racing in 1994. His two sons, Michael and Jeff, and nephew, John, carry on the Andretti winning tradition in auto racing.

Reading

1. Mario and his brother had interesting childhood experiences. In twenty-five words or more, write about a childhood memory of yours that you think your classmates might find interesting.
2. Read about the Indianapolis 500 car race in a reference book. Bring five interesting facts about the race to your classmates.
3. Go through your local newspaper and cut out a picture of the fastest or best car you can find. If possible, get advice from an adult. Tell your friends why you chose the car you did.
4. List three reasons you would feel safe driving across the United States with Mario Andretti as your driver.

Social Studies

1. On a map, find these places mentioned in the biography: Trieste, Italy; Florence, Italy; Lucca, west of Florence; and Nazareth, in eastern Pennsylvania, located above Bethlehem.
2. Pretend you are a race car driver in the last two miles of the Indianapolis 500. Write what you are feeling physically and mentally as you look for the checkered flag indicating you are the winner.
3. Make a list of what you think are the five most dangerous sports. Compare and discuss your list with those of your classmates.

Further Reading

Andretti, Mario. *Andretti.* San Francisco, CA: Collins Publishers, 1994.

Burchard, Marshall. *Sports Hero: Mario Andretti.* New York: G. P. Putman's Sons, 1977.

De Vere, Charles. *Let's Look Up Racing Cars.* New York: Gloucester Press, 1992.

Dolan, Edward F., Jr. *Great Moments in the Indy 500.* New York: Franklin Watts, 1982.

Krishef, Robert K. *The Indianapolis 500.* Minneapolis, MN: Lerner Publications, 1974.

The Lincoln Library of Sports Champions. Volume 1. Columbus, OH: Frontier Press Company, 1993.

Murphy, Jim. *The Indy 500.* New York: Clarion Books, 1983.

Olney, Ross R. *Super Champions of Auto Racing.* New York: Clarion Books, 1984.

Prentzas, G. S. *Mario Andretti.* New York: Chelsea House Publishers, 1996.

Roger Bannister was born in Harrow, England, near London. Ten years later, in World War II, England fought Germany. Roger's family moved to Bath when Germany began bombing London.

Running was the exercise Roger enjoyed most. He was shy and timid and easily frightened by other boys. If confronted by them, he would run. Once he was climbing a tall tree. A friend warned him of the approach of the owner. Roger scurried down and ran, hurtling over a barbed-wire fence that tore his clothing and scratched him. Another time, he was playing with a boat on a pond when a practice air-raid alert was sounded. He ran the half mile home in a panic, believing bombs would fall on him.

The City of Bath Boy's School was made up of young men from the surrounding area and boys evacuated from London. Roger felt part of neither group and described himself as a loner. Basically, he was a very serious young man.

In his autobiography he wrote, "As a boy I had no clear understanding of why I wanted to run. I just ran anywhere and everywhere—never because it was an end in itself, but because it was easier for me to run than to walk. . . . I always felt impatient to see or do something new, and running saved time."

The school had an annual junior cross-country race of three miles. Roger entered and enthusiastically started out at a fast run. He managed to cross the finish line exhausted and eighteenth. When told he should train, Roger did: two and one-half miles twice a week. The next year he won because, as he said, "I refused to let anyone beat me." He won the cross-country race 3 years in a row.

Roger went to Oxford to study medicine in 1946. While there, he was encouraged to take up a sport. Because he was rather frail, running appealed to him. Roger set as his goal the four-minute mile. No one throughout the ages had ever accomplished the feat.

From his studies in medicine, Roger came to the conclusion that running the mile in less than 4 minutes was as much a mental test as a physical one. One runner got as close as 4 minutes and 2 seconds and then declared, "It's a brick wall." Another predicted that Roger would do it because he "uses his brains as much as his legs."

Finally, Roger ran the mile in 3 minutes, 59.4 seconds. The twenty-five-year-old medical student/runner was the first man to complete the mile in less than 4 minutes. Seven weeks later in Turku, Finland, John Landy broke that record. Shortly after, Roger and John raced and both broke the 4-minute barrier with Roger winning. Since then, a number of other runners have lowered the record further.

Roger Bannister received his medical degree in 1954 and won one more race at Bern, Switzerland. He retired from racing to devote his time to a medical life as a neurologist.

Reading

1. Make a list of five words that describe Roger Bannister. Compare your list with those of your classmates. Defend your choices.
2. In a reference book, read what diseases a neurologist treats and report to your classmates what you learned.
3. Share with a classmate what you most admired about Roger Bannister. Why did you choose what you did?
4. Roger's remark, that he refused to let anyone beat him, is a powerful statement. Do you think there may be a negative side to the comment? If so, what would it be?

Social Studies

1. Roger's family took him from London to the city of Bath because of the devastation the German bombing was causing in London. Find the two cities on a map. Which direction did the family travel from London?
2. What direction is Turku from Helsinki, the capital of Finland? What are the two official languages of Finland?
3. Running is sometimes thought of as a solitary activity. What does that mean to you? What sport, in your opinion, would be just the opposite?
4. Pretend you are a journalist covering the meet at which Roger Bannister breaks the 4 minute barrier. Write a headline and a brief article describing this historic moment in track-and-field history.

Further Reading

Bannister, Roger. *The Four-Minute Mile.* New York: Dodd, Mead & Company, 1981.

The Lincoln Library of Sports Champions. Volume 1. Columbus, OH: Frontier Press Company, 1989.

Rosenthal, Bert. *Track and Field.* Austin, TX: Raintree Steck-Vaughn, 1994.

Savage, Jeff. *Running.* Parsippany, NJ: Crestwood House, 1995.

Sullivan, George. *Great Lives: Sports.* New York: Charles Scribner's Sons, 1988.

Wright, Gary. *Track & Field: A Step-by-Step Guide.* Mahwah, NJ: Troll Associates, 1990.

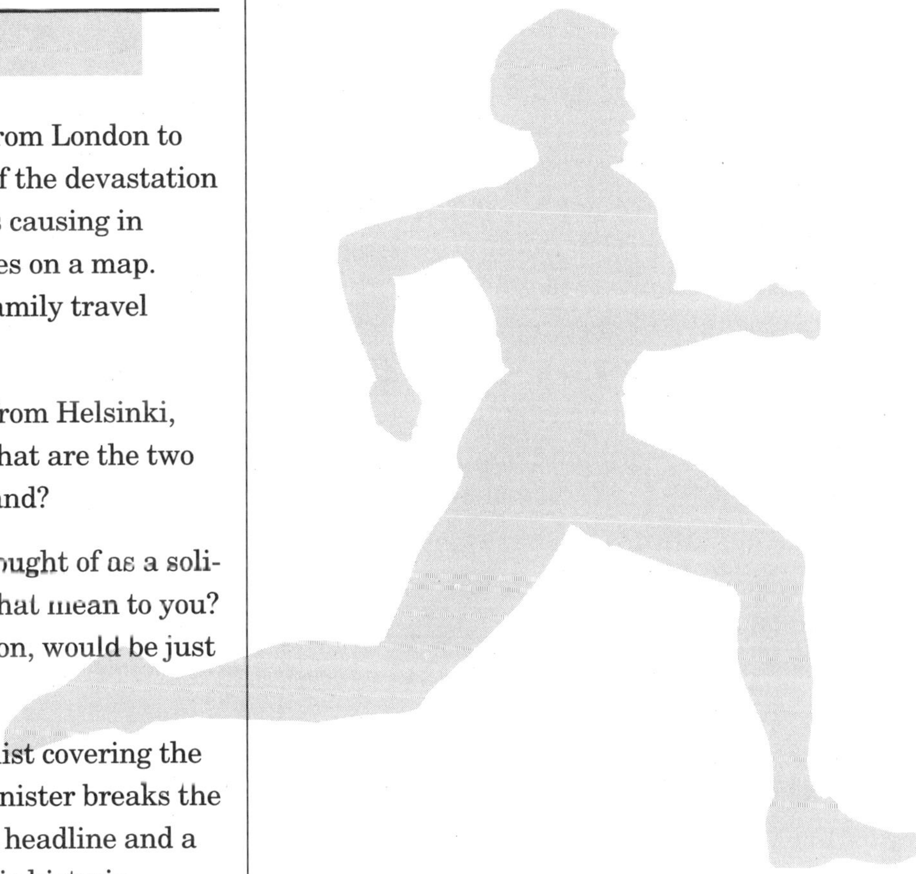

Bonnie Blair

Skating was a family affair for the Blairs, even before Bonnie was born. When her mother, Eleanor, was ready to go to the hospital to give birth to Bonnie, her father, Charlie, was not sure what to do. Three of the children were waiting in the car. They were scheduled to race at an ice skating rink and Charlie was to be a timer. Eleanor decided that she should be dropped off at the hospital first and the rest would proceed to the rink. After all, it might be some time before the baby would come. Later, while they were at the rink, a loudspeaker announcement was made that another skater had just been born into the Blair family. What a surprise! Back to the hospital they raced.

When Bonnie was two, her parents slipped a pair of skates over her shoes. Soon Bonnie was racing other children on weekends with the family. When the Blairs moved to Champaign, they spent much of their time on the ice skating rink at the University of Illinois. The children won national speed skating titles. At age four, Bonnie began winning races.

In 1979 Cathy Priestner, a Canadian silver medalist speed skating champion from Canada, moved to Champaign. Cathy met Bonnie and became her coach. They practiced in the early mornings. Fifteen-year-old Bonnie just missed making the 1980 U.S. Olympic speed skating team.

Bonnie started her career as a pack skater. In pack skating, everyone lines up together in a pack and races to see who will be first to cross the finish line. Bonnie learned to get a quick start. Then she changed to Olympic-style racing. In this type of racing, skaters race against the clock.

More practice was needed by Bonnie on Olympic-sized ice rinks. Since there were few in the United States, she decided to go to Europe to train. This, of course, would take money. Her father was retired and could not help her, so Bonnie went to the local police department for help. The police held bake sales and raffles and collected donations. Finally she had money to travel, practice, and even compete in the World Cup speed skating events. In 1984 she qualified for the U.S. Olympic team!

To gain strength, Bonnie lifted weights, cycled, ran, and carried an inner tube filled with 30 pounds of sand around the track! Because she was participating in so many meets, she did her homework in hotel rooms, automobiles, and during any free time at the ice skating rinks.

Bonnie's relatives, the Blair Bunch, ranging in age from a four-month-old nephew to an 80-year-old uncle, became her personal cheering section at meets. At the 1994 Winter Olympics in Lillehammer, Norway, 60 Blairs showed up.

Just before turning thirty-one, Bonnie retired as the fastest U.S. women's speed skater. She was the first American woman to ever win consecutive Winter Olympic titles. Overall, Bonnie won five gold medals and one bronze in the Olympic games.

Reading

1. Before a race, Bonnie felt best if she ate a peanut butter and jelly sandwich. What is your favorite snack? Is it as nutritious as Bonnie's?
2. Choose a classmate for a writing partner. Each of you write a sentence telling what you like best about Bonnie Blair. Exchange your sentences and write the reason you agree or disagree with your partner's sentence.
3. Write Bonnie's last name vertically on a paper. Use each letter of her name to begin words describing her. Consult a dictionary if you need help. Then do the same with your name, using words that describe you.
4. An alliteration (repeating the same initial consonant sound in two or more words) was used to describe Bonnie: Bonnie Blur. Write two about yourself and share them with your classmates or parents.

Social Studies

1. In the Olympics of 1988, 1992, and 1994, Bonnie won gold medals at Calgary, Canada; Albertville, France; and Lillehammer, Norway. Find these places on a map or globe. What continents are they on?
2. On a map, find Champaign, Illinois, the location of the University of Illinois. What is your favorite college or university? Find it on a map.
3. Bonnie turned down a dinner with the president of the United States because she had to practice for the Winter Olympics in 1988. Who was president at that time? Who was president before him? After him?
4. Often the fans would sing, "My Bonnie Lies Over the Ocean" when Bonnie Blair competed. What is the rest of the first verse of the song? Sing it with your classmates.

Further Reading

Arnold, Caroline. *The Olympic Winter Games.* New York: Franklin Watts, 1991.

Blair, Bonnie with Greg Brown. *A Winning Edge.* Dallas, TX: Taylor Publishing, 1996.

Breitenbucher, Cathy. *Bonnie Blair: Golden Streak.* Minneapolis, MN: Lerner Publications, 1994.

Daly, Wendy. *Bonnie Blair: Power on Ice.* New York: Random House, 1996.

Italia, Bob. *Bonnie Blair: Five-Time Gold Medal Winner.* Edina, MN: Abdo & Daughters, 1994.

Kent, Zachary. *U.S. Olympians. Cornerstones of Freedom.* Chicago, IL: Childrens Press, 1992.

The Lincoln Library of Sports Champions. Volume 2. Columbus, OH: Frontier Press Company, 1993.

MacLean, Norman. *Ice Skating Basics.* Englewood Cliffs, NJ: Prentice-Hall, 1984.

Rambeck, Richard. *Bonnie Blair.* New York: The Child's World, 1996.

McMane, Fred and Cathrine Wolf. *Winning Women.* New York: Bantam Books, 1995.

Susan loved animals from childhood. When she was four, a dog that was part Labrador retriever named Cabee came into her life. As she walked through her neighborhood in Cambridge, Massachusetts, with Cabee, neighborhood dogs would follow along with them. Susan began to understand the emotions they were feeling by just listening to their barking.

By the time she was seventeen, Susan had left the northeast part of the country for Colorado. There she began veterinary training and learned how to care for animals. The annual Iditarod race in Alaska was just beginning and news of it attracted Susan's attention. Alaska beckoned and she left to go to the "top of the world."

In Alaska, Susan purchased three Alaskan huskies. A bush pilot flew her into the Alaskan wilderness with her dogs. Flying was the only way in or out unless one walked on snowshoes. She was by herself with her dogs. She killed wild animals for food, built a cabin, and began training for the 1,000-mile Iditarod Trail Sled Dog Race.

The race was named for a village along an Alaskan trail. This trail played an important role in Alaska's history. In 1925 the children in Nome, Alaska, were exposed to the deadly disease of diphtheria called the "Black Death." Only a serum would save them.

The nearest place the serum was available was in Anchorage, Alaska, 1,000 miles away. Time was running out. Two children had already died. The Bering Sea was frozen. The only airplanes were in storage for the winter. Even if they could be put together in time, the planes were windowless and the pilot might freeze and lose the serum. A train could take the serum 300 miles. The rest of the trip required dog sleds to carry the serum through the cold, windswept Alaskan wilderness. The dog sleds were the only solution.

Dog sled drivers worked in relays along the trail. The temperatures dropped to -50° and the wind blew up to 50 miles an hour. The serum arrived, and many children lived because of the courage and strength of the dogs and the men who drove the sleds. The Iditarod race is held in their honor.

Susan competed in her first Iditarod in 1978 and came in nineteenth. She kept entering and improving year by year. By 1985, she thought she had a good chance of winning with the splendid dogs she had raised. But a huge, starving moose stood in the trail and attacked her team of dogs. One died and thirteen were badly hurt. She had to withdraw.

The next year she won the Iditarod; it was the first of four wins for her. Among Susan's many honors and awards were the 1987 U.S. Sports Academy Female Athlete of the Year and France's Outstanding Female Athlete of the World in 1989.

Reading

1. Read about the plant and animal life in Alaska. Report to your classmates five interesting facts you learned.
2. Read about dogs in an encyclopedia or reference book. In your opinion, what is the most unusual, and the most beautiful, type of dog? Discuss your answers with your classmates.
3. What thoughts and emotions went through Susan's mind when she and her dog team came face-to-face with the starving moose? Write a paragraph describing what she might have felt.
4. After reading the biography of Susan Butcher, what thought came to your mind? Write about it and share it with your classmates.

Social Studies

1. The highest mountain in North America is in central Alaska. What is its name?
2. The Bering Strait separates what country from Alaska?
3. Susan trained alone in the Alaskan wilderness with her dogs. What equipment would you need to survive in the wilderness? What skills would be necessary?
4. What direction is Nome from Anchorage?

Further Reading

Crisman, Ruth. *Racing the Iditarod Trail.* New York: Dillon Press, 1993.

Dolan, Ellen M. *Susan Butcher and the Iditarod Trail.* New York: Walker and Company, 1993.

Gil, Shelley. *Kiana's Iditarod.* Homer, AK: Paws IV Publishing Company, 1984.

Heinrichs, Ann. *America the Beautiful: Alaska.* Chicago, IL: Childrens Press, 1991.

Johnston, Joyce. *Alaska.* Minneapolis, MN: Lerner Publications, 1994.

The Lincoln Library of Sports Champions. Volume 3. Columbus, OH: Frontier Press Company, 1993.

Osborn, Kevin. *Scholastic Encyclopedia of Sports in the United States.* New York: Scholastic, 1997.

Paulsen, Gary. *Woodsong.* New York: Bradbury Press, 1990.

Shahan, Sherry. *Dashing Through the Snow: The Story of the Jr. Iditarod.* Brookfield, CT: The Millbrook Press, 1997.

Thompson, Kathleen. *Alaska.* Austin, TX: Raintree Steck-Vaughn, 1996.

Wood, Ted. *Iditarod Dream: Dusty and His Sled Dogs Compete in Alaska's Jr. Iditarod.* New York: Walker and Company, 1996.

Woolum, Janet. *Outstanding Women Athletes: Who They Are and How They Influenced Sports in America.* Phoenix, AZ: The Oryx Press, 1992.

Jennifer Capriati was on tennis courts before she was born. Her mother, Denise, was receiving tennis instruction from her husband, Stefano, just 17 hours before Jennifer entered this world. Stefano was convinced his new 11-pound daughter would be a future tennis star. Stefano joked that Jennifer was born holding a tennis racket.

Before Jennifer could walk, she was climbing to the top of the monkey bars on the playground. A few months later she was playing with the tennis balls behind the machine that shot balls out for tennis practice. By the time she was four, Jennifer began hitting tennis balls on her own with a small racket.

Stefano played soccer in Milan, Italy, until he was injured. He then went to Spain as a movie stunt man and met Denise, a Pan-American flight attendant, whom he married. They moved to the United States so their first child, Jennifer, would be born as an American citizen. Jennifer's early aptitude for tennis prompted them to move to Lauderhill, Florida. They asked Jim Evert, Chris Evert Lloyd's father, to instruct Jennifer in tennis. He said no. He insisted that a child must be at least five years old to begin tennis lessons. Stefano asked him to watch her play before making a final decision. He did, and was impressed. Jim Evert told his daughter, Chris, that he'd found someone with the kind of tennis potential she had had as a child.

One of Jennifer's problems as a young tennis player was finding competition to sharpen her skills. She beat everybody, including older men and boys. At twelve, she won the eighteen-and-under clay court championship. Another problem was finding time for homework while she played in various tournaments around the country. This was solved by working with a private tutor. She faxed her homework assignments back and forth to her high school teachers at the private school in which she was enrolled.

Practicing tennis was not a problem. She practiced without complaint.

Jennifer joined the professional ranks as a tennis player the month she turned fourteen, and she was the youngest person in the United States ever to do so. In one year in the early 1990s, she won $300,000, not counting her multimillion-dollar endorsement deals for skin care and other products. Her picture appeared on the covers of *Sports Illustrated* and *Newsweek*.

Jennifer had to be careful not to overtrain and burn out. As a precaution, her parents involved her in a strength program to avoid possible serious injuries. Weight lifting, stretching exercises, massage, long daily runs, and wind sprints, coupled with 3 hours of tennis and school work, made up her day.

The high point in her tennis life came when she played Steffi Graf in the 1992 Olympic Games in Barcelona, Spain. After three grueling sets, Jennifer emerged the victor, taking home a gold medal.

Reading

1. Compare and contrast Jennifer's biography with the biographies of other tennis players. How are they alike or different? Who is your favorite? Why?

2. Create three titles for the biography of Jennifer Capriati. Arrange them in your order of preference. Compare yours with those of your classmates.

3. Draw three cartoon pictures of Jennifer: first, as a child climbing the monkey bars; second, hitting tennis balls as a four-year-old; and third, standing on a platform receiving the gold medal in Barcelona, Spain.

4. Visit a tennis court when it is empty. In a paragraph, write what you see. Then imagine you are playing against a famous tennis player and the bleachers are filling up with tennis fans. Write how you feel and how well you play. Share your paragraphs with a friend.

Social Studies

1. Locate Milan, Italy, and Barcelona, Spain, on a map or globe. Read about these two famous cities in a reference book and report three interesting facts about each one to your classmates.

2. To maintain health, daily exercise is important for old and young alike. Make a list of your daily exercises or physical activities and compare it with those of your classmates. If practical, discuss what you learned with your health or physical education instructor.

3. Pretend you are featured on the covers of *Sports Illustrated* and *Newsweek* magazines. How would you handle this experience? How would your friends react to your fame? Write an essay of fifty to seventy-five words about how you feel.

4. When she had free time, Jennifer enjoyed going to shopping malls with her high school friends. Make a list of places in your community you would take Jennifer, if she visited you. Compare your list with those of your classmates.

Further Reading

Gutman, Bill. *Jennifer Capriati: Teenage Tennis Star.* Brookfield, CT: The Millbrook Press, 1993.

Goldstein, Margaret J. *Jennifer Capriati: Tennis Sensation.* Minneapolis, MN: Lerner Publications, 1993.

Lakin, Patricia. *Jennifer Capriati: Rising Star.* Vero Beach, FL: Rourke Enterprises, 1993.

Miller, Marc. *Fundamental Tennis*. Minneapolis, MN: Lerner Publications, 1995.

Morrissette, Mikki. *Jennifer Capriati*. New York: Little, Brown and Company, 1991.

Singleton, Skip. *The Junior Tennis Handbook: A Complete Guide to Tennis for Juniors, Parents, and Coaches.* Cincinnati, OH: Shoe Tree Press, 1991.

Woolum, Janet. *Outstanding Women Athletes: Who They Are and How They Influenced Sports in America*. Phoenix, AZ: The Oryx Press, 1992.

Roberto Clemente

1934-1972 • Baseball

In northeast Puerto Rico lies the city of Carolina. There Roberto Clemente was born to Melchor and Luisa Clemente. The family lived close to the sugar cane fields where Melchor worked for $2 a week. Even when he was promoted to foreman at $4 a week, there was little money to spare.

At nine, Roberto wanted a bicycle. His father told him to earn it. So Roberto took a job carrying an empty milk can for a neighbor to a grocery store about a half mile away. The grocer filled it with milk and Roberto carried it back. For this chore he received a few cents a day. When he was twelve, he had earned enough money to buy a used bicycle.

Playing ball was Roberto's great passion. With an old tree limb, he hit tin cans and balls made of tightly bound rags. At night he squeezed a rubber ball to strengthen his hands. By the time he was eighteen, he signed a contract to play for the Puerto Rican Winter League. His $500 signing bonus, plus $60 a week and a new mitt, seemed like a dream come true.

In November 1954, the Pittsburgh Pirates chose Roberto in the major league draft. But tragedy followed. His oldest brother, Luis, died of a brain tumor on New Year's Eve. Then Roberto was in a near fatal automobile crash when a drunken driver plowed into his car. Roberto's spinal cord was damaged. This injury bothered him for some time.

Things looked better when he met Vera Cristina Zabala, who worked at a bank. She did not know he was the famous Puerto Rican baseball player until her friends from work saw him and told her. Nevertheless, Vera's family followed the custom that young people must be chaperoned when dating. They were married in 1963 and had three sons.

As a baseball player, Roberto became noted for his fielding, hitting, and throwing. In 1966 he was named the National League's Most Valuable Player. In his last game in the major leagues, in 1972, Roberto needed one hit to become the eleventh player in history to get 3,000 hits. He succeeded!

For some time, Roberto planned a recreation center (Sports City) between San Juan and Carolina for the children of the island. They needed a free place to play.

On December 23, 1972, an earthquake in Nicaragua killed 7,000 people and left many injured and homeless. Roberto was named the Puerto Rican honorary relief chairman. To make sure that the medicines and food got to the people, he decided to go there and supervise its distribution. On New Year's Eve, 1972, the supply plane carrying him and a few others crashed off the coast of Puerto Rico. All were killed.

The five-year waiting period for induction into the Baseball Hall of Fame was lifted. Roberto was enshrined a few weeks later, the first Puerto Rican to be honored. People contributed to Roberto's recreation center. It became a memorial to a young man who began by hitting homemade cloth balls with a tree limb.

Reading

1. In what particular sport or occupation would you like to excel? Make a list of five important things to do to be the best in that sport or occupation. Sit in a circle with a few friends and read and respond to each other's lists.
2. What is your opinion about having an older brother, sister, or parent as a chaperone when dating? What do you like about this custom?
3. From the biography, copy two sentences that indicate Roberto's determination to make himself a success in baseball. Share and compare your sentences with your classmates.
4. Who among your friends has the potential to be a professional athlete? Why?

Social Studies

1. Find Puerto Rico on a map or globe. Then find Carolina, the city where Roberto Clemente was born.
2. Find Nicaragua on a map or globe. What country lies to its north? South? What body of water lies to its east? West?
3. Earthquakes are most often caused by movement of the Earth. What is this movement called?

Further Reading

Bjarkman, Peter C. *Roberto Clemente.* New York: Chelsea House Publishers, 1991.

Dunnahoo, Terry Janson and Herma Silverstein. *Baseball Hall of Fame.* New York: Crestwood House, 1994.

Geng, Don. *Fundamental Baseball.* Minneapolis, MN: Lerner Publications, 1995.

Green, Carol. *Roberto Clemente: Baseball Superstar.* Chicago, IL: Childrens Press, 1991.

Gutelle, Andrew. *Baseball's Best: Five True Stories.* New York: Random House, 1990.

Kalb, Jonah. *How to Play Baseball Better Than You Did Last Season.* New York: Macmillan Publishing Co., 1974.

Krull, Kathleen. *Lives of the Athletes: Thrills, Spills (and What the Neighbors Thought).* New York: Harcourt, Brace & Company, 1997.

The Lincoln Library of Sports Champions. Volume 4. Columbus, OH: Frontier Press Company, 1993.

Macht, Norman L. *Roberto Clemente.* New York: Chelsea Juniors, 1994.

O'Connor, Jim. *The Story of Roberto Clemente: All-Star Hero.* Milwaukee, WI: Gareth Stevens Publishing, 1995.

Walker, Paul Robert. *Pride of Puerto Rico: The Life of Roberto Clemente.* San Diego, CA: Harcourt Brace Jovanovich, 1988.

Ty Cobb grew up wanting two things: to win every contest he entered and to please his father. Pleasing his father was difficult. His father, nicknamed "the Professor," had high goals for Ty. He wanted Ty to be a doctor, lawyer, or perhaps an army officer. Ty's goal was to be a professional baseball player.

When he was 17, Ty had the opportunity to try out for a minor league team. Summoning his courage, he asked his father if he could leave home for a tryout. His father talked to him until three o'clock in the morning, telling him of his need for a college education and the riffraff in baseball with whom he would associate. Ty could only counter with, "I just have to go."

Finally, Professor Cobb wrote out six checks for $15, each with a different date for cashing, and the admonishment to "get it out of your system." When Ty didn't make the team, he called home to tell his father that he had an opportunity with another team. Expecting the worst, Ty was happy to hear his father say, "Don't come home a failure." Ty made the roster of the next club.

Just before Ty moved into the big leagues, Ty's mother accidentally killed the Professor when she thought he was a robber entering their home through a window late at night. It was then Ty learned his father carried newspaper clippings of his earliest feats on the baseball field. He was very proud of Ty.

Ty's fierce determination to be the best often cost him not only the friendship of those on opposing teams, but also the friendship of his own team members. He spent much time alone visiting public libraries, art galleries, and museums, even operas and classical concerts.

When he developed a fever and it was diagnosed as inflamed tonsils, Ty found a doctor who would remove them without anesthesia. He felt he could not miss appearing in the lineup or someone else would take his place. A friend carried him to bed after the operation. In great pain, he played the next day. The doctor was committed to an asylum for the insane shortly after the operation.

In 1906 Ty began a hitting streak in which he batted .320 or higher every year for 23 years. In 1911 he hit .420 for the year and was voted the most valuable player in the American League. In 1915 he began a major league record for the most stolen bases: 892. That record lasted 47 years.

Despite his success, his temper got in his way. Once he jumped into the stands and beat up a fan who was yelling insults. Ty was suspended for 10 days and fined $50.

Ty invested his money wisely in a copper mine, in General Motors stock when it was first offered, and a company called Coca-Cola. During World War I, he enlisted in the U.S. Army and served as a captain in the Chemical Warfare Service. In 1936 the first group of players was inducted into the Baseball Hall of Fame. Ty got more votes than any other player, including Babe Ruth, and became the first inductee to be honored.

Reading

1. After reading the biography of Ty Cobb, and another book or reference about him, make a list of three titles that best depict his life.
2. What thought or idea in the biography surprised you? Explain the surprise to your parents or classmates.
3. As you read about Ty Cobb, in what ways are you similar to and different from him? List the ways in two columns headed Alike and Different.
4. Rank the following in order of importance to you: (1) a player's batting average for the year, (2) his number of home runs in a year, or (3) his base hits in a year. Defend your position with your classmates.

Social Studies

1. Do you think Ty would have been equally as successful as a lawyer or doctor if he had chosen one of these professions rather than baseball? Why?
2. Babe Ruth was noted for hitting home runs, Ty Cobb for getting base hits and stealing bases. Which of these two types of players do you think is more important to the success of a baseball team? Explain your opinion to your classmates.
3. Imagine Ty Cobb visiting your home for dinner. Who among your friends and relatives (limit of five, not including yourself) would you invite? Why?
4. At this time, who is your favorite baseball player in the major leagues? On what team does he play? In a reference book, read about the city in which he plays, and report three things of interest about the city to your classmates.

Further Reading

Dunnahoo, Terry Janson and Herma Silverstein. *Baseball Hall of Fame*. New York: Crestwood House, 1994.

Geng, Don. *Fundamental Baseball*. Minneapolis, MN: Lerner Publications, 1995.

Jacobs, William Jay. *They Shaped the Game: Ty Cobb, Babe Ruth, Jackie Robinson.* New York: Charles Scribner's Sons, 1994.

Kalb, Jonah. *How to Play Baseball Better Than You Did Last Season.* New York: Macmillan Publishing Co., 1974.

The Lincoln Library of Sports Champions. Volume 3. Columbus, OH: Frontier Press Company, 1993.

Macht, Norman L. *Ty Cobb*. New York: Chelsea House, 1992.

Osborn, Kevin. *Scholastic Encyclopedia of Sports in the United States.* New York: Scholastic, 1997.

Sullivan, George. *Great Lives: Sports.* New York: Charles Scribner's Sons, 1988.

The small town of Onesti nestles in the Moldavian Carpathian Mountains of eastern Romania. When Nadia Comaneci was six years old, she and a friend were doing their "exercises" in a school yard of Onesti. Nadia loved to skip and jump and run and move like the wind. At the side of the yard, a man and a woman watched Nadia in fascination. They were gymnastics coaches who were constantly on the lookout for children with gymnastic potential. Then the bell rang and Nadia and her friend disappeared into the school before the couple could talk to them.

The coaches, Bela and Marta Karolyi, went through the school twice looking for the two girls. But the Karolyis could not recognize them. The third time around, Bela asked the question, "Who loves gymnastics?" The two girls raised their hands excitedly. Nadia went on to train with the Karolyis, and her friend became a ballerina.

Two years later, Nadia won the Romanian national junior gymnastics title. By the time she was fourteen, she was in international competitions. Nadia won gold medals in London, England; Oslo, Norway; and at the American Cup competition in New York City.

Bela Karolyi said Nadia had a number of characteristics that made her skillful in gymnastics. They were strength, agility, speed, intelligence, and concentration. To top it off, he said she possessed great courage. It did take courage to do back flips on a 4-inch narrow board high above the floor and to twist and turn on the uneven parallel bars, especially if you were only 5 feet tall and weighed 86 pounds!

What truly set the stage for Nadia's popularity in gymnastics was the performance of a young girl from the Soviet Union, Olga Korbut. In the 1972 Olympics in Munich, Germany, Olga won three gold medals and a silver. She became the spokesperson for gymnastics. The sport gained enormous popularity, especially in the United States.

In 1976 Nadia made Olympic history at the games in Montreal, Canada. Seven times she earned scores of 10. In the Olympics, a 10 in gymnastics competition is a perfect score. She earned her gold medals competing in exercises on the uneven parallel bars, the balance beam, and in the all-around competition. She was in ninth grade that year.

By 1979, at 18 years of age, Nadia was 5 feet 3 1/2 inches tall and weighed 106 pounds. The following year the Olympics were held in Moscow. Nadia won gold medals in the balance beam and the floor exercise competitions.

She retired from competitive gymnastics and began coaching Romanian youth. The Romanian communist government put travel restrictions on her, so Nadia left Romania and toured with a group of gymnasts. She and an American gymnast, Bart Conner, fell in love and married and now live in Colorado.

Reading

1. Nadia's coach said she had strength, agility, speed, intelligence, concentration, and courage. Rank these characteristics in order of importance. Compare your ranking with those of your classmates. How do you differ? Discuss your reasoning with each other.
2. Does Nadia remind you of someone you know? Who? In what way?
3. Using a recent almanac, skim over the various competitions at the Olympic Games. What surprised you most? Compare your findings with those of your friends or relatives.

Social Studies

1. With two or three friends, find the following places where Nadia lived, or traveled to, as an athlete: The mountains of the Moldavian Carpathians; Onesti, Romania; Oslo, Norway; London, England; Moscow, Russia; Montreal, Canada; Munich, Germany.
2. Choose two locations from the cities and countries above and read about them in a reference book. With your classmates, discuss three of the most interesting things you learned.
3. When did Communist Romania hold its first free multiparty elections after World War II?
4. What incident in the biography reminds you of something that happened to you? Relate it to two friends or a parent.

Further Reading

Bragg, Linda Wallenberg. *Fundamental Gymnastics*. Minneapolis, MN: Lerner Publications, 1995.

Brodman, Jonathon, editor. *Athletes*. Volume 2. Danbury, CT: Grolier 1996.

Burchard, Sue H. *Sports Star, Nadia Comaneci*. New York: Harcourt Brace, 1977.

Cohen, Joel H. *Superstars of Women's Gymnastics*. Philadelphia, PA: Chelsea House Publishers, 1997.

Grumeza, Ian. *Nadia*. New York: Hawthorn Books, 1977.

Haycock, Kate. *Gymnastics*. New York: Crestwood House, 1991.

Jones, Betty Millsaps. *Wonder Women of Sports*. New York: Random House, 1981.

The Lincoln Library of Sports Champions. Volume 4. Columbus, OH: Frontier Press Company, 1993.

McMillam, Constance Van Brunt. *Nadia Comaneci: Enchanted Sparrow*. St. Paul, MN: EMC Corporation, 1977.

Readhead, Lloyd. *The Fantastic Book of Gymnastics*. Brookfield, CT: Copper Beech Books, 1997.

Sullivan, George. *Great Lives: Sports*. New York: Charles Scribner's Sons, 1988.

__________. *The Picture Story of Nadia Comaneci*. New York: Julian Messner, 1977.

Woolum, Janet. *Outstanding Women Athletes: Who They Are and How They Influenced Sports in America*. Phoenix, AZ: The Oryx Press, 1992.

New York City was hot in the summer, so Gertrude Ederle, nicknamed Trudy, went to the pool to keep cool. Her parents owned a cottage in New Jersey. It was there that Trudy's father taught her to swim when she was eight years old. Later, at 15, she got a membership in the Women's Swimming Association on Manhattan's lower East Side. The lessons she took there improved her natural ability to swim.

Trudy soon won national swimming titles in 200- and 400- yard races. Then she tried longer races. In a 3-mile race she beat fifty world-class swimmers. At 17, she set 18 world distance records.

Trudy decided to attempt a long swim from the Battery in lower New York City, across New York Bay, and on to Sandy Hook New Jersey, a distance of 21 miles. With one mile to go, the outgoing tide began to slow Trudy down. Her sister, riding in a boat nearby, began scolding her and telling her she was loafing. This upset Trudy, so she tried harder to finish. She not only accomplished her goal, but broke the men's record besides.

The 1924 Olympic Games in Paris beckoned Trudy. For the second time, women were allowed to compete in swimming. In France, she won two bronze medals. As lead-off swimmer in the 400-meter women's relay, she won the gold along with three other young women.

The challenge that really excited Trudy was not at the Olympics. It was one no woman had ever attempted: swimming the 21-mile English Channel. Many men had tried, but only five had succeeded. On Trudy's first attempt to cross, the strong current forced her to quit because she attempted to go too fast.

In a later attempt, Trudy set off from the French coast at 7:09 in the morning. Her body was layered with olive oil, then a coat of lanolin, and another covering of lard and petroleum jelly. The current was too strong for a rowboat escort, so a tugboat stayed beside her. A coach encouraged her to keep a steady pace, and she set off for the coast of England.

Trudy became seasick. Because of the waves and cold she lost her hearing. Many people rooted for her. Along the coast of England, people lit bonfires as their welcome. That night, August 6, 1926, Trudy finally walked ashore. She reached Dover at 9:40 P.M., approximately 14 hours after she started. Her time was 2 hours faster than any of the five men who had swum the English Channel before her. Asked by a reporter how she felt, she replied, "Wet."

Two million New Yorkers turned out to welcome the now-famous teenager with a traditional ticker-tape parade. Commercial endorsement contracts totaling $200,000 were offered her. This was a tremendous amount of money at that time. A few years later, Trudy fell in her New York apartment and injured her spine. It took 4 years for her to recover. After that she taught deaf children to swim. Trudy made swimming a major sport for women.

Reading

1. Does Gertrude Ederle remind you of someone you know? Who? In what way?
2. Share with a classmate two things you admire most about Gertrude Ederle.
3. Do you know a location that is 21 miles from where you live? If so, think about places where you could stop to rest if the road was one long swimming channel. How many rest stops would you have to make? Where would you stop?

Social Studies

1. On a map, trace the swimming route Gertrude Ederle took from Battery Park on lower Manhattan, through Upper and Lower New York Bay, to Sandy Hook, New Jersey. What large island was west of her most of the time she was swimming?
2. What bodies of water does the English Channel connect?
3. At the English Channel's narrowest part, what English and French cities are opposite each other?
4. Read about New York City in a reference book. What three things about the city interest you most? Share them with your classmates.

Further Reading

Dabney, Gene. *Swimming: A Step-by-Step Guide.* Mahwah, NJ: Troll Associates, 1990.

Gorton, Eddie. *Swimming.* London: Batsford Academic and Educational Ltd., 1982.

The Lincoln Library of Sports Champions. Volume 5. Columbus, OH: Frontier Press Company, 1993.

Krull, Kathleen. *Lives of the Athletes: Thrills, Spills (and What the Neighbors Thought).* New York: Harcourt, Brace & Company, 1997.

Orr, C. Rob and Jane B. Tyler. *Swimming Basics*. Englewood Cliffs, NJ: Prentice-Hall, 1980.

Osborn, Kevin. *Scholastic Encyclopedia of Sports in the United States*. New York: Scholastic, 1997.

Sandelson, Robert. *Swimming and Diving.* New York: Crestwood House, 1991.

Verrier, John. *Swimming and Diving.* Crystal Lake, IL: Rigby Education, 1996.

Wilson, Charlie G. *Swimming and Diving.* Morristown, NJ: Silver Burdett Press, 1987.

Chris Evert was the second of five children. Her father, Jim, played tennis for the University of Notre Dame. After graduation, he became a tennis instructor and manager of a tennis complex in South Florida. Tennis was a family affair. All the children played tennis and all became good at it.

Jim noticed how hard Chris hit tennis balls against a wall, before she was 6 years old, so he started giving her lessons. As Chris grew older, she practiced 20 hours a week after school and on weekends. Off the court she was shy, but on the court Chris relentlessly hit the ball across the net until her opponents made a mistake. Because she was a child and didn't have the strength of older players, Chris worked hard to develop a powerful two-handed backhand for returning the ball. When she was behind in tennis matches, she would battle to win. Her endurance, developed from constant practice, made her a winner.

In 1970 the tennis world found out what a top-flight player she was. Margaret Court, about 10 years older than Chris, had just won the Grand Slam—four of the top tennis tournaments in the world. Only one person had done it before Margaret, and Chris beat Margaret when Chris was only fifteen!

The day Chris turned eighteen, she turned professional and signed a $50,000 contract endorsing tennis wear. The media created nicknames describing her style of play as "Little Miss Cool" and "Ice Princess."

The interest she generated in tennis brought many young girls into the sport. The publicity brought the media to her doorstep. Her father and mother tried to keep family life as normal as possible. Her father finally told the journalists that came to the Evert house that he didn't want to be rude, but the children needed their rest, all five of them, and they did have homework to do.

In 1976 *Sports Illustrated* named Chris Sportswoman of the Year, the first woman to be chosen for the honor. The Associated Press honored her as the Female Athlete of the Year several times. At one point, she had a winning streak of 125 straight matches on clay courts. Chris had 157 singles titles, 1,300 career match wins, and from 1972 to 1989 was never below the top-four ranking for women in tennis.

By the time Chris was 28, she was worth $10,000,000. Even so, she had been taught by her parents to make wise purchases. So when she decided to buy an expensive car, she had her husband call to find out what her father might say. Of course, she had the money to buy several cars. Someone said, in jest, that she could start a car dealership with the cars she won as prizes in tournaments.

Chris was the first professional tennis player to win 1,000 matches. Over her 19-year career she averaged .903 wins. She retired in 1989 and analyzed tennis matches for television.

Reading

1. After reading the biography of Chris Evert, close the book and list five important things you remember about her. Share your list with classmates or friends. Were any items on your list the same as those of your classmates?

2. Often short biographies leave a reader feeling there is much more to learn about a person. What more would you like to know about Chris Evert? Make a list with a friend and see if you can find out the answers by reading more about her.

3. List the names of two older relatives or adult friends whom you think would enjoy this biography. Read the biography to them and discuss their reactions to what you read.

4. With a highlighter pen, highlight three sentences that you think tell something important about Chris. Discuss your choices with your classmates.

Social Studies

1. Make a list of four products you could comfortably endorse. Write a sentence or two why you believe in each of these products. Discuss with your classmates.

2. What four counties form the southern tip of Florida? What city is farthest south? What is the name of the large national park located in South Florida?

3. What character traits must a person like Chris Evert need to be a consistent winner in her sport for 19 years? Make a list and discuss it with a small group of classmates.

4. After discussing question 3, make a list of those character traits you already have and a list of those you desire to attain.

Further Reading

Aaseng, Nathan. *Winning Women of Tennis.* Minneapolis, MN: Lerner Publications, 1981.

Hahn, James and Lynn. *Chris! The Sports Career of Chris Evert Lloyd.* Mankato, MN: Crestwood House, 1981.

The Lincoln Library of Sports Champions. Volume 5. Columbus, OH: Frontier Press Company, 1993.

MacCurdy, Doug and Shawn Tully. *Sports Illustrated Tennis.* New York: Harper & Row, 1980.

May, Julian. *Chris Evert: Princess of Tennis.* Mankato, MN: Creative Education Society, 1977.

O'Shea, Mary Jo. *Winning Tennis Star: Chris Evert.* Mankato, MN: Creative Education Society, 1977.

Schmitz, Dorothy Childers. *Chris Evert: Women's Tennis Champion.* Mankato, MN: Crestwood House, 1977.

Schwabacher, Martin. *Superstars of Women's Tennis.* New York: Chelsea House Publishers, 1997.

Smith, Jay, H. *Chris Evert.* Mankato, MN: Creative Education Society, 1975.

Woolum, Janet. *Outstanding Women Athletes: Who They Are and How They Influenced Sports in America.* Phoenix, AZ: The Oryx Press, 1992.

Lou Gehrig

1903-1941 • Baseball

On June 19, 1903, a big baby boy of 14 pounds was born to Heinrich and Christina Gehrig in New York City. The couple had emigrated from Germany, met in New York City, married, and worked hard to make a living for themselves and their child. They named him Heinrich Ludwig Gehrig, but he became known to all as Lou Gehrig.

Lou's favorite gift as a child was a baseball catcher's mitt he got for Christmas when he was five. It was for a boy who threw with his right hand and Lou was left-handed. After Lou caught the ball, he tucked the mitt under his right arm and threw with his left. Lou didn't mind because he knew his parents were poor and sacrificed a lot to get it for him.

The chubby boy grew to be strong. When Lou was eleven, he swam across the Hudson River, a distance of one mile. His father was proud of him but boxed his ears for taking such a chance with his life.

By the time he went to Commerce High School, the shy young man weighed 200 pounds. He played sandlot baseball, football, and soccer. One of his teachers heard he was a good baseball player. The teacher told him to go to the next high school baseball game and play. When he got there, he heard the crowd roaring, so he immediately went back home. He was too timid to be in front of a crowd. His teacher threatened to fail him if he didn't join the team. So he did.

Lou hit a home run in the ninth inning of a championship game for his high school and was featured in the newspaper. That brought him offers to play for college teams. His mother and father were delighted that he could go to college, but they had little money and his father was ill and out of work.

To pay the bills, Lou's mother got a job cooking in a fraternity house while Lou was at Columbia University. Even so, Lou worked, too. He served meals at the fraternity house.

While in college, Lou played football and baseball. Then his mother contracted double pneumonia and the family was months behind in making its rent payments. When the New York Yankees offered him a contract for $3,500 for the remaining months of the 1923 season, he took it to help his family.

Babe Ruth was the star for the Yankees at that time. With Bob Meusel, Lou, and the Babe, the Yankees had three .300 hitters in a row. They were called Murderer's Row. Opposing pitchers had difficulty getting them out.

In 1933 Lou married Eleanor Twitchell, who helped him to overcome his lack of self-confidence. Lou played day after day during the 1930s, never missing a game. Then in 1938, he went into a slump. He couldn't hit or move the way he had. On May 2, 1939, he benched himself after 2,130 consecutive games. At the Mayo Clinic in Minnesota, he was diagnosed with a disease called amyotrophic lateral sclerosis (ALS), and he died at age 37.

Reading

1. Does Lou Gehrig remind you of someone you know? Who? In what way?
2. When Lou Gehrig found out he was dying of an incurable disease, he said that he still considered himself "the luckiest man on the face of the Earth." Why do you think he felt this way? Explain.
3. How many hits would a .300 hitter get if he or she batted 100 times? One thousand times?
4. From the biography, read aloud three sentences that best tell about the kind of person Lou Gehrig was. Read them to a classmate or parent.

Social Studies

1. What is amyotrophic lateral sclerosis (ALS), and what is this disease called today?
2. The Mayo Clinic in Minnesota is one of the world's largest medical centers. Read about it in a reference book. Report to your class or parents three interesting facts you learned. In what city is it located? Find it on a map.
3. What is your favorite professional baseball team? On a map, locate the place where it plays its home games.
4. What is the name of the baseball player, and his team, who surpassed Lou's record of most consecutive games played?

Further Reading

Adler, David A. *Lou Gehrig: The Luckiest Man.* New York: Harcourt, Brace & Company, 1997.

Brandt, Keith. *Lou Gehrig: Pride of the Yankees.* Mahwah, NJ: Troll Associates, 1986.

Dunnahoo, Terry Janson and Herma Silverstein. *Baseball Hall of Fame.* New York: Crestwood House, 1994.

Geng, Don. *Fundamental Baseball.* Minneapolis, MN: Lerner Publications, 1995.

The Lincoln Library of Sports Champions. Volume 6. Columbus, OH: Frontier Press Company, 1993.

Luce, Willard and Celia. *Lou Gehrig: Iron Man of Baseball.* Champaign, IL: Garrard Publishing Company, 1970.

Kalb, Jonah. *How to Play Baseball Better Than You Did Last Season.* New York: Macmillan Publishing Co., 1974.

Macht, Norman L. *Lou Gehrig.* New York: Chelsea House Publishers, 1992.

Osborn, Kevin. *Scholastic Encyclopedia of Sports in the United States.* New York: Scholastic, 1997.

Rambeck, Richard. *Lou Gehrig.* Chicago, IL: The Child's World, 1994.

Althea Gibson was born to sharecroppers in Silver, South Carolina. In 1930, after sharing their cotton crop with the landowner, they made only $75 for the whole year. Mr. Gibson went to New York City and got a job as a handyman in a garage at $10 a week, and his family joined him later. They lived in an apartment in Harlem, the black section of the city.

Althea did not care much for school and often missed classes. Sometimes she rode the subway throughout the night because she was afraid to go home and face her father. Although he loved her, he whipped her, hoping to make her obey. It didn't work.

To defend herself when she was traveling alone, he gave her boxing lessons. One day, with one punch, Althea flattened a man who was beating his wife.

The Police Athletic League put wooden barricades on Althea's street so the children could have a summer playground. Althea excelled at paddle ball and won trophies. Buddy Walker, whose regular work as a musician was slow in the summer months, worked for the city as the playground leader. He bought Althea two secondhand tennis rackets and taught her tennis.

She played so well that two African American medical doctors, who were interested in promoting African American tennis players, took her into their families. Althea lived with Dr. Hubert Eaton of Wilmington, North Carolina, and his family during the school year. She practiced on his tennis court and continued her high school education. In the summer, she lived with Dr. Robert Johnson's family in Lynchburg, Virginia. He took her and others on the all-black American Tennis Association tour. She won its championship title 10 years in a row. Finally, she stopped, "to give somebody else a chance," she said.

Althea received an athletic scholarship to Florida A & M University in Tallahassee. She played on the tennis and basketball teams.

Tennis star Alice Marble believed that Althea should be allowed to play in the all-white United States Lawn Tennis Association tournaments. She wrote in the USLTA journal that people in the association were acting like "sanctimonious hypocrites" by keeping her out on the basis of race. Althea was finally given the chance to play in the USLTA based on her ability. In 1950 she became the first African American to compete in the national championships at Forest Hills.

The U.S. State Department sent Althea and three other U.S. players on a goodwill tour of Thailand, Burma (Myanmar), Pakistan, India, Indonesia, and Malaysia in Southeast Asia. In 1957 she became the first African American player to win at Wimbledon.

After her tennis career, Althea joined the Ladies Professional Golf Association as a pro golfer. The talented young woman also acted with John Wayne in the movie *The Horse Soldiers.* Later she became the Recreation Director for the City of East Orange, New Jersey.

Reading

1. Write the names of three relatives who would enjoy the biography of Althea Gibson. Tell why you chose each person and plan to read it to at least one of them.
2. Write a short essay of approximately 50 words telling why whipping a child helps or does not help him or her to want to obey.
3. Pretend Althea came to your class. Write three questions you would ask her. See if you can find any of the answers in the books listed for Further Reading, or use others in your library.
4. Check a dictionary for the words *sanctimonious* and *hypocrites*. Write a definition of this phrase in simple words and compare it with those of your classmates.

Social Studies

1. Compare biographies of Jackie Robinson and Althea Gibson. How are they alike? How are they different?
2. Alice Marble believed that Althea should be judged by ability rather than the color of her skin. What special beliefs do you have? Share them with your classmates and discuss them.
3. List the countries in Southeast Asia that Althea and the other tennis players visited on the goodwill tour. Choose one and find five interesting facts, in a reference book, to share with your classmates.

Further Reading

Aaseng, Nathan. *Winning Women of Tennis.* Minneapolis, MN: Lerner Publications, 1981.

Biracree, Tom. *Althea Gibson: Tennis Champion.* Los Angeles, CA: Melrose Square Publishing Company, 1990.

Davidson, Sue. *Changing the Game: The Stories of Tennis Champions Alice Marble and Althea Gibson.* Seattle, WA: Seal Press, 1997.

Gibson, Althea and Edward E. Fitzgerald. *I Always Wanted to Be Somebody.* New York: Harper & Row, 1958.

Jones, Betty Millsaps. *Wonder Women of Sports.* New York: Random House, 1981.

The Lincoln Library of Sports Champions. Volume 6. Columbus, OH: Frontier Press Company, 1993.

Singleton, Skip. *The Junior Tennis Handbook: A Complete Guide to Tennis for Juniors, Parents, and Coaches.* Cincinnati, OH: Shoe Tree Press, 1991.

Woolum, Janet. *Outstanding Women Athletes: Who They Are and How They Influenced Sports in America.* Phoenix, AZ: The Oryx Press, 1992.

When Steffi Graf was three years old, she watched her father play tennis. She exclaimed she would like to play tennis just like he did. So her father, Peter Graf, cut the handle off a tennis racket so Steffi could hold it.

Peter, an automobile dealer and insurance salesman, loved to play tennis. Her mother, Heidi, also played well. Steffi and her dad played tennis in the house, causing disorder with the furniture. They moved to the downstairs playroom after smashing some lamps. Peter set up chairs as a net. He promised her breadsticks if she could return his volleys several times in a row without missing. She became so good that he had to raise the number of times she had to do it without missing.

Her father sold his dealership when Steffi was five years old. The family moved from Mannheim, Germany, to a small town called Bruhl. There he opened a tennis club and Steffi began playing on a real tennis court. Peter became her coach and Steffi became an outstanding tennis player at a very young age.

By the time she was 12, Steffi was winning tournaments in competition with players older than she. Trophies and prizes began to fill the home of the Grafs. Peter decided it was time for Steffi to begin competing against adult women tennis players, since she already ranked so highly with them inEurope.

At 13, Steffi dropped out of eighth grade and turned professional. Peter hired a personal school tutor to travel with them to tournaments all over the world. In 1984, when she was fifteen, Steffi journeyed to Los Angeles for the Summer Olympics. Tennis was not yet an official sport at the Olympics. It was called a "demonstration" sport. Even so, Steffi won the gold medal.

Steffi continued to win tournaments and earn money. She worked hard to be the very best. She exercised, lifted weights, and practiced her serve, forehand, and backhand drive for long hours every day. Her opponents were amazed at her powerful forehand when she sent the ball back over the net. Coupled with her astonishing foot speed, Steffi kept her competition off balance.

Steffi especially wanted to win the Grand Slam of tennis. This meant winning the four major tournaments of the year: The Australian Open, French Open, Wimbledon (in England), and the United States Open. In 1988, this finally happened when she was 19 years old. And that same year she won an Olympic gold medal. This put her in the history books. No man or woman had ever done that!

In 1993 she won $2,753,000, bringing her total at that time to more than $13,000,000. But money was not that important. She was in Chicago for a tournament and it was cold. She called her father. He laughed and told her to buy herself a coat. She had millions of dollars!

Steffi Graf retired in 1999.

Reading

1. Think back to the first game you ever played. How old were you? What was the game? Compare your experience with that of your friends.
2. Steffi did not have time to be with her friends when she became a professional tennis player. Write a paragraph about something you had to give up in order to gain something else of value.
3. What does the word *ace* mean in tennis talk?
4. If you could ask Steffi one question about her career in tennis, what would it be?

Social Studies

1. Two rivers meet near Mannheim, Germany, where Steffi was born. What are they?
2. To win the Grand Slam of professional tennis, a player must win tournaments in four different countries. What are the countries? Find them on a map or globe.
3. What Olympic sport and its event is of most interest to you? In a reference book, read about the winner of that event in the last Olympics. Share what you find out with your classmates.

Further Reading

Brodman, Jonathon, editor. *Athletes.* Volume 2. Danbury, CT: Grolier, 1996.

Brooks, Philip. *Steffi Graf: Tennis Champ.* New York: Childrens Press, 1996.

Hilgers, Laura. *Steffi Graf.* New York: The Time Inc. Magazine Company, 1990.

Knapp, Ron. *Sports Great Steffi Graf.* Springfield, NJ: Enslow Publishers, 1995.

The Lincoln Library of Sports Champions. Volume 7. Columbus, OH: Frontier Press Company, 1993.

MacCurdy, Doug and Shawn Tully. *Sports Illustrated Tennis.* New York: Harper & Row, 1980.

McMane, Fred and Cathrine Wolf. *Winning Women.* New York: Bantam Books, 1995.

Miller, Marc. *Fundamental Tennis.* Minneapolis, MN: Lerner Publications, 1995.

Rothaus, James R. *Steffi Graf.* Chicago, IL: The Child's World, 1991.

Schwabacher, Martin. *Superstars of Women's Tennis.* New York: Chelsea House Publishers, 1997.

Singleton, Skip. *The Junior Tennis Handbook: A Complete Guide to Tennis for Juniors, Parents, and Coaches.* Cincinnati, OH: Shoe Tree Press, 1991.

Woolum, Janet. *Outstanding Women Athletes: Who They Are and How They Influenced Sports in America.* Phoenix, AZ: The Oryx Press, 1992.

Wayne's father gave him his first pair of skates when he was two years old. Walter Gretzky had played junior hockey in Canada, but he now worked for the telephone company. He built Wayne a skating rink in the backyard by flooding it with water and letting it freeze. Wayne's mother turned on the lawn sprinkler from time to time to water the 40-by-60-foot rink in order to keep it smooth for Wayne to practice on.

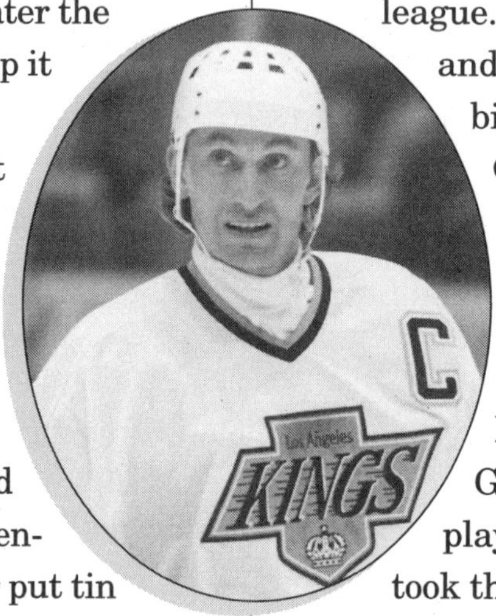

Walter cut down the smallest hockey stick he could find so his son could practice shooting a hockey puck into a net. Sometimes he would put a table in front of the net with just enough room on the sides so Wayne could aim the puck into the narrow openings and make a goal. His father put tin cans, traffic cones, and hockey sticks on the rink. Wayne skated around them as he swiftly moved the puck with his hockey stick up and down the rink. At night, lights were set up in the backyard for Wayne to continue practicing. Wayne loved to play. In fact, he wanted to join the youth league at five, but the league had a rule that a youngster must be six to play.

By the time Wayne was 10 years old he was 4 feet 4 inches tall and weighed 70 pounds. In the Peewee games he made 378 goals in 68 games. Newspapers and television stations interviewed him. Some of the parents were upset because their children weren't able to make goals because of Wayne, but he did pass off to the other children frequently.

Wayne performed well in other sports, also. He was a fast sprinter, good at lacrosse, and an excellent baseball player. A major league baseball team offered him a contract even though he'd signed with a professional hockey team. But hockey was his first love.

In order to have stronger competition, Wayne went to Toronto and lived with a family there so he could play in a more advanced league. At 17, he turned professional and, eventually, on his eighteenth birthday, he joined the Edmonton Oilers.

His fans called him "The Great Gretzky," imitating the title of a book by F. Scott Fitzgerald, *The Great Gatsby.* His idol over the years was Gordie Howe, a tremendous hockey player who wore number 9. Wayne took the number 99 and made that number famous.

Wayne began to break the records that great hockey players had set for many years. At age 19 he was the youngest player to receive the Hart Memorial Trophy as the most valuable player in the National Hockey League. He continued receiving the trophy for the next 7 years.

In 1988 he asked to be traded to the Los Angeles Kings in the United States so he could move to be with his wife, an actress there. But in 1992 he awoke one night with severe back pain caused by a herniated disk. It was doubtful that he would ever play again. Wayne fought back. He exercised and went on to win more awards, becoming the most outstanding hockey player in the world. Wayne Gretzky retired from professional hockey in 1999.

Reading

1. Read other biographies and books about Wayne Gretzky. Make a list of his awards. Which one do you think was the most important to him? Discuss your answer with classmates who also answered this question.
2. With two or three friends role-play a conversation between Wayne, Walter, and his mother concerning the decision about Wayne leaving home and living with a family in Toronto so he could play in a more advanced hockey league.
3. What might have happened if Wayne had gone into professional baseball instead of hockey? Write a paragraph of fifty words or less to explain your answer.

Social Studies

1. From the following list of teams in the National Hockey League, locate the states or provinces in which they are found on a North American map.

   Atlanta Thrashers, Atlanta, GA
   Boston Bruins, Boston, MA
   Buffalo Sabres, Buffalo, NY
   Carolina Hurricanes, Morrisville, NC
   Calgary Flames, Calgary, AB
   Chicago Black Hawks, Chicago, IL
   Colorado Avalanche, Denver, CO
   Columbus Blue Jackets, Worthington, OH
   Dallas Stars, Irving, TX
   Detroit Red Wings, Detroit, MI
   Edmonton Oilers, Edmonton, AB
   Florida Panthers, Sunrise, FL
   Hartford Whalers, Hartford, CT
   Los Angeles Kings, Inglewood, CA
   Mighty Ducks of Anaheim, Anaheim, CA
   Minnesota Wild, St. Paul, MN
   Montreal Canadiens, Montreal, PQ
   Nashville Predators, Nashville, TN
   New Jersey Devils, East Rutherford, NJ
   New York Islanders, Uniondale, NY
   New York Rangers, New York, NY
   Ottawa Senators Hockey Club, Kanata, ON
   Philadelphia Flyers, Philadelphia, PA
   Phoenix Coyotes, Scottsdale, AZ
   Pittsburgh Penguins, Pittsburgh, PA
   St. Louis Blues, St. Louis, MO
   San Jose Sharks, San Jose, CA
   Tampa Bay Lightning, Tampa, FL
   Toronto Maple Leafs, Toronto, ON
   Vancouver Canucks, Vancouver, BC
   Washington Capitals, Landover, MD

2. Choose a Canadian city and a U.S. city from the list of National Hockey League franchises above. Read about each city in a reference book and discuss with your classmates why you would want live in each particular city.
3. What is the name of the trophy that is given annually to the team that wins the National Hockey League championship?

Further Reading

Knapp, Ron. *Top 10 Hockey Scorers.* Hillside, NJ: Enslow Publishers, 1994.

Rappoport, Ken. *Sports Great Wayne Gretzky.* Springfield, NJ: Enslow Publishers, 1996.

Rozens, Aleksandrs. *Wayne Gretzky: Magician on the Ice.* Vero Beach, FL: Rourke Enterprises, 1993.

Sullivan, George. *Great Lives: Sports. Books for Young Readers.* New York: Charles Scribner's Sons, 1988.

Florence Griffith Joyner | 1959–1998 • Track and Field

Florence was the seventh of 11 children. Her parents separated when she was young and her mother took the children to the Watts district of Los Angeles to live. The family was poor and sometimes ate oatmeal three times a day. But there was much love in the family.

Florence's middle name was Delorez and as a child she became known as Dee Dee. Dee Dee loved to run. When she visited her father in the Mojave Desert, she chased jackrabbits. Back in Watts, she became involved in the Sugar Ray Robinson Youth Foundation and took part in organized races. By the time she was 14, she won a track meet sponsored by Jesse Owens, an Olympic champion sprinter.

Mrs. Griffith set rules for her children: bed by 10 P.M. and no television during the week. Dee Dee was an A student in school. She had a mind of her own and had a boa constrictor snake for a pet! Her hobbies included sewing and creating new hair styles for herself and others.

After performing well as a track star and student at Jordan High School in Los Angeles, Florence entered California State University at Northridge. She worked with Bob Kersee, a women's track coach. When he transferred to UCLA, she went there, too, majoring in psychology. She barely missed qualifying for the 1980 Olympic team, but she made it to the 1984 Olympic Games held in Los Angeles. She won a silver medal in the 200-meter run.

Florence became as well known for her long fingernails as she was for her running, for she let them grow to four inches and painted them a variety of colors. For a while she dropped out of running and took a job in a bank, but she returned and graduated from UCLA in 1983.

In 1987 she married Al Joyner, a 1984 Olympic gold medalist. She took the last name of Griffith Joyner, and soon the press called her "Flo-Jo," a combination of her first and last names. Her coach, Bob Kersee, and her husband, Al Joyner, both worked with her in preparation for the 1988 Olympics in Seoul, Korea.

Florence trained diligently, often late into the night. To make faster starts, she lifted leg weights for more than an hour a day. She did 100- and 200-meter sprints and ran about 4 miles a day. She was determined to win a gold medal.

At track meets, her creativity in dress was distinct. Besides the long painted fingernails with rhinestones, birds, and trees on them, she designed track uniforms of various colors and styles. Once she accidently cut off a leg of one uniform, so she ran with one leg bare and the other covered.

In the 1988 Olympics in Seoul, Korea, where wearing the U.S. team uniform was required, she won gold medals in the 100 meters, 200 meters, the 400-meter relay, and a silver medal in the 1600-meter relay. She was "the fastest woman in the world." Flo-Jo died of an epileptic seizure at her home at the age of 38.

Reading

1. To you, what sort of person is Florence Griffith Joyner? Would you have liked to have had her as a friend? Why or why not?
2. Using the biography of Florence, create a comic strip. Create "balloons" for the words she might say. Make at least ten panels. Read and discuss your comic strip with younger children.
3. Florence was known for her personal flair and style as well as for her running ability. What is your personal style? Describe it in a paragraph.
4. Copy what you consider the most important sentence in the biography of Florence Griffith Joyner. Defend your choice against those of your classmates.

Social Studies

1. Find the Mojave Desert on a physical map of California. What direction is Los Angeles from the desert?
2. Are there any incidents or locations in Florence's biography that remind you of something in your life? List them and discuss them with your classmates.
3. A social problem that Florence and her family had to combat early in life was being poor. What social problems do people in your community have to face? What is being done about them? What should be done?
4. Find Seoul, Korea, on a map. What is the approximate north latitude line that separates North and South Korea?

Further Reading

Aaseng, Nathan. *Florence Griffith Joyner: Dazzling Olympian.* Minneapolis, MN: Lerner Publications, 1989.

Hunter, Shaun. *Great African Americans in the Olympics.* New York: Crabtree Publishing Company, 1997.

Kent, Zachary. *U.S. Olympians.* Chicago, IL: Childrens Press, 1992.

Koral, April. *Florence Griffith Joyner: Track and Field Star.* New York: Franklin Watts, 1992.

The Lincoln Library of Sports Champions. Volume 5. Columbus, OH: Frontier Press Company, 1993.

Merrison, Tim. *Field Athletics.* New York: Crestwood House, 1991.

Rosenthal, Bert. *Track and Field.* Austin, TX: Raintree Steck-Vaughn, 1994.

Sandelson, Robert. *Track Athletics.* New York: Crestwood House, 1991.

Savage, Jeff. *Running.* Parsippany, NJ: Crestwood House, 1995.

Stewart, Mark. *Florence Griffith Joyner.* New York: Childrens Press, 1996.

Wickham, Martha. *Superstars of Women's Track and Field.* New York: Chelsea House Publishers, 1997.

Woolum, Janet. *Outstanding Women Athletes: Who They Are and How They Influenced Sports in America.* Phoenix, AZ: The Oryx Press, 1992.

Wright, Gary. *Track & Field: A Step-By-Step Guide.* Mahwah, NJ: Troll Associates, 1990.

Eight-year-old Dorothy Hamill put one skate forward, then the other, on Morse's Pond behind her grandparents' home. She fell, got up again, then smiled. She could skate! A group of children went by, skating backward. But skating backward didn't work for her, for Dorothy fell down. Then she got right back up and began again.

Dorothy spent the winter skating near her home in Rye, New York, wearing out her first pair of skates in the process. Because she loved to skate, her mother decided Dorothy should have lessons.

Her first competition was in New York City's Central Park. She did well. Her father began a notebook listing events she entered and the results. There were notebooks for her sister and brother, too. They contained lists of each child's flu shots, grades, and other achievements.

Soon it was obvious that Dorothy could be a medal-winning figure skater. But that meant sacrifice on her part as well as that of the rest of the family. She had to go to places where there were ice rinks. This required getting up at 5 o'clock in the morning, six days a week. She learned to eat, sleep, and study in the car. It also meant getting to bed by 7 or 8 o'clock in the evening to be ready to start her practice schedule again in the morning.

The family made sacrifices, too. The car required gas and oil. The lessons were expensive. Her mother gave up things she wanted to do. Dorothy had to travel to other parts of the country so she could train with excellent coaches. The expenses became enormous. Her commitment to the goal of becoming the best figure skater in the world also meant she couldn't participate in school activities as others did. But her love for skating meant more to her.

One September she was at Lake Placid, New York, with her coach, Gustave Lussi. He suggested she try something new for her routine, a flying camel layover. Dorothy added another move by dropping into a sit spin. Newspapers later called it the "Hamill Camel."

Sometime later, Dorothy went to Denver, Colorado, to train and practice with another coach, Carlo Fassi. There she finished high school at the Colorado Academy. After graduation, she spent more than two hours every morning at the ice rink. Dorothy ate breakfast, jogged and exercised, skated in the afternoon, and then again in the late afternoon. If she went out in the evening, she had to be back by 9 o'clock.

The Winter Olympics began on February 4, 1976, in Innsbruck, Austria. All the years of hard work and competitions paid off. Nineteen-year-old Dorothy was selected to represent the United States and received the figure skating gold medal. A few weeks later she won the World Championship in Göteborg, Sweden. Dorothy turned professional and joined the Ice Capades for 3 years. She later married a sports medicine specialist named Ken, and they had a little girl, Alexandra.

Reading

1. Name one personal characteristic Dorothy Hamill had that made her a successful figure skater. On a scale of 1 to 10, what number would you give yourself for that particular characteristic?
2. Have you ever had to make a sacrifice in order to gain something in the long run? Write a paragraph about it. Was it worth it?
3. Pretend you are a reporter interviewing Dorothy after she won her Olympic gold medal. What would be your first question? What would her answer be?
4. Why would you like, or not like, to be a younger brother or sister of Dorothy Hamill?

Social Studies

1. Read in a reference book about Innsbruck, Austria. Tell your classmates what you learned. Show them where it is located on a map or globe.
2. Of all the places listed in the biography, where would you prefer to go for a vacation? Why?
3. Create a drawing of Dorothy doing a Hamill Camel. Write a caption below the picture.
4. Write a sentence of twenty words or less telling why you would or would not want to make a living as a figure skater.

Further Reading

Arnold, Caroline. *The Olympic Winter Games.* New York: Franklin Watts, 1991.

Gutman, Dan. *Ice Skating: From Axels to Zambonis.* New York: Viking, 1995.

Hamill, Dorothy with Elva Clairmont. *On and Off the Ice.* New York: Alfred A. Knopf, 1983.

Hilgers, Laura. *Great Skates.* Boston, MA: Little, Brown and Company, 1991.

The Lincoln Library of Sports Champions. Volume 5. Columbus, OH: Frontier Press Company, 1993.

MacLean, Norman. *Ice Skating Basics.* Englewood Cliffs, NJ: Prentice-Hall, 1984.

Osborn, Kevin. *Scholastic Encyclopedia of Sports in the United States.* New York: Scholastic, 1997.

Ryan, Margaret. *Figure Skating.* New York: Franklin Watts, 1987.

Sanford, William R. and Carl R. Green. *Dorothy Hamill.* New York: Crestwood House, 1993.

Smith, Pohla. *Superstars of Women's Figure Skating*. Philadelphia: Chelsea House Publishers, 1997.

Van Steenwyk, Elizabeth. *Dorothy Hamill: Olympic Champion.* New York: Harvey House Publishers, 1976.

Woolum, Janet. *Outstanding Women Athletes: Who They Are and How They Influenced Sports in America.* Phoenix, AZ: The Oryx Press, 1992.

Sonja Henie was born during a snowstorm in Oslo, Norway, on April 8, 1912. Her brother, Leif, was 5 years older than she. Her mother, Selma, and father, Wilhelm, both came from wealthy families. Wilhelm had inherited a fur business, and the royalty of Europe wore his furs.

Wilhelm was athletic as a youth, winning world bicycle championships and excelling in speed skating. As he grew older, he became a financial genius. But his family, and especially Sonja, took priority over everything else.

As a child, Sonja followed her brother everywhere he went, even ice skating. When she was five, Sonja went out on the ice with skates that clamped onto her shoes and won her first skating contest. The first-place prize was a silver-handled paper cutter, which she put under her pillow for luck. Now it rests in a museum in Oslo with many of her other trophies.

Her father bought her an expensive pair of shoe skates. He also made sure that she got the best ice skating teachers. By the time she was 10, she jumped from Junior Class C competition to Senior A and won the Norwegian ladies title. Her daily schedule included practicing 3 hours in the morning and 2 hours in the afternoon. Her classes in ballet influenced the way she skated. At 11, she went to the 1924 Olympic Games at Chamonix, France, the first Winter Olympics. She came in last, but one judge ranked her first in free skating. Wilhelm was infuriated that she had not won a medal.

The next Winter Olympics, in St. Moritz, Switzerland, were quite different. Sonja not only won the gold medal in figure skating, but she won the hearts of the crowds. Her style of skating was more like ice dancing and included twists and turns and flowing glides. Also, her costumes were much different from those of the other skaters. They wore long skirts and dark colors. Sonja's skirts were short and trimmed with fur.

After the 1928 Olympics, Sonja decided that her long-range goal was to be a movie star. She planned to make herself known as a figure skater and then move to Hollywood. With her father's backing, she put on ice skating performances everywhere, and won gold medals in the 1932 Olympics at Lake Placid, New York, and again in 1936 in Garmisch-Partenkirchen, Germany. Finally, she turned professional and put on an ice show in Hollywood so movie producers could see her.

Sonja Henie became the movie star she planned, plus more. When she wasn't making a movie, she was performing on ice everywhere. After one movie featured her skating in white ice skates, all the stores in the United States sold out of them in one week. Sonja became a U.S. citizen. By 1956, she retired from ice skating and married Nils Onstad. They built a museum in Oslo to hold their art collection and Sonja's trophies. She died of leukemia at the age of 57.

Reading

1. Sonja won gold medals in figure skating in three different Winter Olympic games. Without rereading the biography, try to recall the countries in which these games took place. Then reread the biography to see if you were correct.
2. Read the biography of Sonja Henie to an older person, perhaps a grandmother or grandfather. When you are finished, ask what he or she remembers about her.
3. Write a dialogue with Sonja's white skates. What would you say and ask them? What would they say and ask you?
4. Sonja's goals included becoming a world-class figure skater and a movie star. Make a list of some of your long-term goals. Then describe the steps you would need to take to make each goal happen.

Social Studies

1. Chamonix, France, is just east of southern Switzerland and northern Italy. Find it on a map.
2. Find Oslo, Norway, on a map or globe. Read about the city in a reference book or text. Share with your classmates five interesting things you learned. Did any of them choose the same items as you did? If so, which ones?
3. Write a nonrhyming poem about the Winter Olympics. Select a setting from any one of the Olympic sites from 1928 to the present (find the list in a reference book). Read in a reference book about the site you chose and refer to it in your poem.
4. Draw a picture of Sonja skating in her fur-trimmed skating outfit among those young women with long skirts of dark colors.

Further Reading

Aaseng, Nate. *Great Winter Olympic Moments.* Minneapolis, MN: Lerner Publications, 1990.

Arnold, Caroline. *The Olympic Winter Games.* New York: Franklin Watts, 1991.

Gutman, Dan. *Ice Skating: From Axels to Zambonis.* New York: Viking, 1995.

Hilgers, Laura. *Great Skates.* Boston, MA: Little, Brown and Company, 1991.

Knight, Theodore. *The Olympic Games.* San Diego, CA: Lucent Books, 1991.

Krull, Kathleen. *Lives of the Athletes: Thrills, Spills (and What the Neighbors Thought).* New York: Harcourt, Brace & Company, 1997.

The Lincoln Library of Sports Champions. Volume 8. Columbus, OH: Frontier Press Company, 1993.

Lindop, Laurie. *Athletes.* New York: Henry Holt and Company, 1996.

Ryan, Margaret. *Figure Skating.* New York: Franklin Watts, 1987.

Tames, Richard. *The Modern Olympics.* Crystal Lake, IL: Rigby Education, 1996.

Smith, Pohla. *Superstars of Women's Figure Skating.* New York: Chelsea House Publishers, 1998.

Woolum, Janet. *Outstanding Women Athletes: Who They Are and How They Influenced Sports in America.* Phoenix, AZ: The Oryx Press, 1992.

Sir Edmund Hillary

Edmund Hillary was born in Auckland, New Zealand. He loved to read, especially adventure stories. His father was very strict and made bed checks at night to make sure his children were sleeping. Ed tied a string to his toe and ran it down the hall to the room of his sister, June. When their father passed June's room, she pulled on the string and Edmund knew to turn out his light and pretend to sleep.

When he was 16, Ed went with his class to visit Mount Ruapehu, south of Auckland. He was entranced with the mountain and with snow. He hiked on weekends with his sister and her friends and read every book he could find on mountain climbing. Every chance he had, he went mountain climbing and learned much about the sport. At home, Ed worked with his father caring for his hundreds of beehives.

At the outbreak of World War II, Ed joined the Royal New Zealand Air Force as a navigator. After the war, he returned to mountain climbing and became a member of a team of New Zealanders exploring the southwestern side of Mount Everest, the highest mountain in the world. It stands at 29,028 feet above sea level between Nepal and Tibet. At that time, no one had ever been able to climb to its top, for the air at that altitude has little oxygen and breathing is difficult at that height.

The leader of the expedition teamed Ed with Tenzing Norgay, a Sherpa native of Nepal. Hundreds of Sherpa men and women porters carried 50 to 60 pounds of supplies apiece during the three-week trek to the base camp. As the teams went up the mountain, they stopped at designated sites and set up camp stations. This allowed the teams to get warm and eat. The higher they went, the more they needed the oxygen containers they carried. Because the sun was bright, glancing off the snow, the members of the expedition wore dark glasses to avoid blindness.

Edmund Hillary and Norgay were chosen to make the last effort to scale the top of Mount Everest. That night Ed's boots froze. He had to thaw them before they could go on. As they climbed, they said little in order to conserve their energy and prevent unstable ice giving way beneath them. A fall would be two miles down. After wedging themselves through a crack in the ice, they reached the top together. It was 11:30 A.M., May 29, 1953.

The two men received many honors from their countries and others around the world. They became good friends. Ed's love for the people of the high Himalayas was demonstrated by his launching of construction projects for schools, hospitals, clinics, airfields, and bridges for his mountain friends.

Ed returned home to marry Louise Rose under an archway of ice axes. Ed became the first man to reach the South Pole on a tractor adapted to that terrain. He studied the effects of high altitudes on humans. He searched for the Abominable Snowman, or yeti, as the Sherpas called it. But to the Sherpas, he was fondly remembered as the man who built schools for their children.

Reading

1. What kind of person was Sir Edmund Hillary? Make a list of his traits from reading the biography and one or more books about him from the Further Reading list. Discuss your thoughts with your classmates.
2. The tallest office building in the world is the Petronas Towers in Malaysia (1,483 feet). What is the tallest building in the United States? Where is it located? (See a reference book.)
3. A 2-mile fall off Mount Everest is how many feet? How many feet higher is Mount Everest than the Petronas Towers?
4. Draw a picture of Edmund Hillary and Tenzing Norgay at the top of Mount Everest. Beneath the picture, write what you imagine the two men might have said to each other when they reached the top.

Social Studies

1. "It is not the mountain we conquer, it is ourselves. If you can overcome your fear, you are frequently able to extend yourself far beyond what you normally regard as your ability." What does this quote by Sir Edmund Hillary mean to you? Discuss your answer with your classmates or parents.
2. New Zealand is made up of two islands. What are their names? On which island was Edmund born?
3. Approximately how many miles above sea level were Hillary and Norgay when they stood together at the top of Mount Everest?
4. The south geographic pole near the center of Antarctica is the point where invisible lines circling the Earth meet. What are these lines called?

Further Reading

Davidson, Bob. *Hillary and Tenzing Climb Everest.* New York: Dillon Press, 1993.

Foster, Lynne. *Take a Hike! The Sierra Club Kid's Guide to Hiking and Backpacking.* Boston, MA: Little, Brown and Company, 1991.

Fraser, Mary Ann. *On Top of the World: The Conquest of Mount Everest.* New York: Henry Holt and Company, 1991.

Gaffney, Timothy T. *Edmund Hillary: First to Climb Mt. Everest.* Chicago, IL: Childrens Press, 1990.

Hacking, Sue Muller. *Mount Everest and Beyond: Sir Edmund Hillary.* New York: Marshall Cavendish, 1997.

Hunt, Sir John and Sir Edmund Hillary. "Triumph on Everest." *National Geographic 106* (1954): 1-64.

Krull, Kathleen. *Lives of the Athletes: Thrills, Spills (and What the Neighbors Thought).* New York: Harcourt, Brace & Company, 1997.

The Lincoln Library of Sports Champions. Volume 8. Columbus, OH: Frontier Press Company, 1989.

Skinner, Todd and John McMullen. *Modern Rock Climbing: Beyond the Basics.* Merrillville, IN: ICS Books, 1993.

Stewart, Whitney. *Sir Edmund Hillary: To Everest and Beyond.* Minneapolis, MN: Lerner Publications, 1996.

Michael Jordan's dad made the comment that two-and-a-half-year-old Michael played with a stick in his hand or bounced a ball all the time. Later, in grade school, he played short stop and pitcher for a Little League Baseball team. He was nicknamed "Rabbit" because of his quickness.

Michael's older brother, Larry, made the varsity basketball team as a senior in high school. Michael was disappointed because he didn't make it as a tenth grader. He went home crying and his mother cried with him. But his disappointment led him to practice harder and longer. Michael looked up to his older brother and it wasn't long before he could beat him one-on-one in backyard basketball. He grew even taller than Larry. When Michael did make the varsity team, he chose the number 23, because it was about half of 45, his brother's number.

Michael's father was also his inspiration. Mr. Jordan had a way of sticking his tongue out when he worked with his tools. Michael picked up the habit and did the same thing when he went for a basket. It became his trademark.

The summer before his senior year in high school, Michael went to a summer camp for high school basketball players. He waited on tables to pay his way. Michael found he could compete with the top high school players around the country.

Michael's high school coach brought him to school at six in the morning so he could practice a couple of hours before classes. He practiced after school with the team and on weekends. He was suspended from school when he skipped classes to go to the gym for more practice time. Finally his father asked if he wanted to play college basketball. If he did, he would have to study so he could get admitted to college. Michael got the message. He graduated from Laney High School in Wilmington, North Carolina, in 1981 with a game average of 28 points and 12 rebounds.

He decided to play for coach Dean Smith of the Tar Heels at the University of North Carolina in Chapel Hill. He was a starter as a freshman. In the last game for the NCAA title, Michael was given the ball for the final shot. From 16 feet out, the ball sailed through the air and into the basket. North Carolina won 63–62! On campus, Michael was called the "Last Shot."

Michael skipped his senior year of college and turned professional. Later he returned in the off-season to get his degree in geology. But before he joined the Chicago Bulls, he went to the 1984 Olympics in Los Angeles and won a gold medal in basketball. He went on to lead the Bulls to their first NBA championship in 1992.

Even so, not everything went well for Michael. His beloved father was murdered in 1993. Michael retired from basketball in 1994 to become a professional baseball player with the Birmingham Barons, a farm team of the Chicago White Sox. Later he returned to the Chicago Bulls and continued to set new basketball records. In 1999 he again retired from basketball.

Reading

1. When Michael switched athletic careers in 1994 to play baseball, he said, "I can accept failure, but I can't accept not trying." What do you think he meant by this statement?
2. What are the meanings of these acronyms? NCAA, NBA
3. What are the nicknames for three of your favorite teams? Write them down and compare them with your classmates' favorites.
4. In what ways are basketball and baseball alike and different?

Social Studies

1. Michael Jordan endorses a number of different products. With two other classmates, make a list of the products you see or hear him advertise.
2. Find Chapel Hill on a North Carolina map. What large city is just northeast of Chapel Hill? What large city is southeast of it?
3. With two friends, create a new sports game that would involve four to six players. Describe the object of the game, the rules, and how the game is won.
4. Some professional basketball players make a great deal of money in their sport. Make a list telling why this is good and bad. Talk with some adults and get their reactions, too. Discuss with your classmates the pros and cons.

Further Reading

Brooks, Philip. Michael Jordan: *Beyond Air.* Chicago, IL: Childrens Press, 1995.

Christopher, Matt. *Michael Jordan.* Boston: Little, Brown and Company, 1996.

Deegan, Paul J. *Michael Jordan: Basketball's Soaring Star.* Minneapolis, MN: Lerner Publications, 1988.

Dolan, Sean. *Michael Jordan: Basketball Great.* New York: Chelsea House Publishers, 1994.

Italia, Bob. *Michael Jordan.* Edina, MN: Abdo & Daughters, 1992.

Knapp, Ron. *Michael Jordan: Star Guard.* Hillside, NJ: Enslow Publishers, 1994.

__________. *Top 10 Basketball Scorers.* Sports Top 10. Hillside, NJ: Enslow Publishers, 1994.

The Lincoln Library of Sports Champions. Volume 9. Columbus, OH: Frontier Press Company, 1993.

Lipsyte, Robert. *Michael Jordan: A Life Above the Rim.* New York: HarperCollinsPublishers, 1994.

Rothaus, James R. *Michael Jordan.* Chicago, IL: The Child's World, 1991.

Joan Mary Joyce enjoyed spending time with her brother on the playground. Her father took the two of them and watched while they played. Mr. Joyce encouraged her to try various sports and she began participating in many of them. By the time she was 13, she had become very good at softball.

Just before the turn of the century, softball was created as an indoor game by George W. Hancock in Chicago. He was a member of a boat club. Because it was often stormy outside, George took an old boxing glove and bound it to make a ball. Then he got a broomstick for a bat and a game was begun in the club's gymnasium. A few years later, the Minneapolis Fire Department, having no fires to fight at the time, took the game outdoors. By the 1930s, the Amateur Softball Association was organized and promoted softball all over the United States. By 1952, there was an International Softball Association.

Today there are two types of pitching in softball: fast pitch and slow pitch. In both, the pitcher throws the ball underhand. Joan threw fast pitch and was clocked at more than 115 miles per hour!

As a young teenager, she played with the Stratford Raybestos Brakettes, a team in Connecticut. Many of their players were eighteen-year-olds. She then went with a California team and, later, came back to Connecticut with a professional softball team. The teams she played for won 19 national championships.

In her career she won 753 games as pitcher. One-hundred and fifty of those games were no-hit, no-run games and 50 were perfect games. As a batter, she also excelled with an average of nearly .325 during her career. These records put her into the National Amateur Softball Hall of Fame.

When Joan pitched the ball, it would go up and down, drop suddenly, and twist, in addition to traveling at great speed. The year after the famous baseball hitter, Ted Williams, retired, he came to Waterbury, Connecticut, and tried to hit her pitches. He was only able to foul a few. He could not connect at all. She struck out another great hitter, Hank Aaron, in 1978, and Hank is the major league's leading career hitter of home runs!

Joan was not only a great softball player, she was also an All-American woman's basketball player at Chapman University in California. During her years playing basketball, she averaged 25 points per game. She also excelled in bowling and volleyball. Upon retiring from softball, she took up golf and joined the Ladies Professional Golf Association (LPGA). Even in golf, she set new records.

In 1994, as Florida Atlantic University's first women's softball coach, her teams set records. She was named the Trans American Athletic Conference Softball Coach of the Year and went on to coach FAU's women's golf team. Joan Joyce is an all-round woman athlete in the tradition of "Babe" Didrickson Zaharias.

Reading

1. Do you know anyone who is like Joan Joyce? How are they like her? How are they different?

2. The acronym LPGA stands for the Ladies Professional Golf Association. An acronym is sometimes sounded out as a word and is formed from the first letters or syllables of a group of words, such as "self-contained underwater breathing apparatus" (SCUBA) or "absent without leave" (AWOL). Find two or three in a newspaper or magazine and write out their meanings.

3. Summarize Joan Joyce's athletic career in exactly 30 words and compare your summary with that of a classmate. How are your summaries alike and different?

Social Studies

1. In a reference book, look up Chapman University and Florida Atlantic University. In what city and state is each located and when was each founded? Locate them on a map. What direction are they from your present location?

2. Choose any sport. Then write an essay of approximately 125 words on what it takes to be a superior coach of that sport.

3. Pretend you are a journalist for your local newspaper. Write a news article about Joan striking out a well-known baseball player with her underhand, fast-pitch softball. Answer the questions who? what? when? where? why? and how?

4. You are sitting by yourself on a bench by a softball diamond. Joan Joyce sits beside you. Make a list of questions you would ask her. Discuss with your classmates ways she might answer the questions.

Further Reading

Craig, Susan and Ken Johnson. *Softball's Power Offense.* Champaign, IL: Sagamore Publishing, 1997.

Galt, Margot Fortunato. *Up to the Plate: The All American Girls Professional Baseball League.* Minneapolis, MN: Lerner Publications, 1995.

Jensen, Julie. *Beginning Softball.* Minneapolis, MN: Lerner Publications, 1997.

Jones, Betty Millsaps. *Wonder Women of Sports.* New York: Random House, 1981.

Joyce, Joan and John Anquillare with Dave Klein. *Winning Softball.* Chicago, IL: Henry Regnery Company, 1975.

Lindop, Laurie. *Athletes.* New York: Henry Holt and Company, 1996.

The Lincoln Library of Sports Champions. Volume 9. Columbus, OH: Frontier Press Company, 1993.

Macy, Sue. *A Whole New Ball Game: The Story of the All-American Girls Professional Baseball League.* New York: Henry Holt and Company, 1993.

Pagnoni, Mario and Geral Robinson. *Softball: Fast and Slow Pitch.* Indianapolis, IN: Masters Press, 1995.

Woolum, Janet. *Outstanding Women Athletes: Who They Are and How They Influenced Sports in America.* Phoenix, AZ: The Oryx Press, 1992.

After Alfred and Mary Joyner, two black teenagers from East St. Louis, Illinois, were married, they had four children. Their second child was a little girl, so her grandmother suggested the name Jackie because she liked Jackie Kennedy, who at that time was the wife of the president of the United States.

Even though the family was poor, the parents worked hard to support them. There were times on cold nights that the family slept in the kitchen to take advantage of the heat coming from the stove. Some nights their dinner consisted of bread smeared with mayonnaise.

Fortunately, the Mary E. Brown Community Center was close by and the children spent much time there. Jackie and her brother Alfred, 2 years older than she, participated in the programs.

Jackie's coach, Nino Fennoy, soon realized that Jackie possessed not only athletic ability but the personality and drive to succeed at a high level in sports. When the Center's teams went to various events, he encouraged her to keep a journal. This he corrected for grammar and spelling.

Jackie's mother, knowing the kinds of trouble her daughter faced in the neighborhood, insisted that she not date until she was 18. And Jackie listened.

By the time she was 12 years old, Jackie could jump as far as 17 feet. That's better than many high school athletes can manage! In 1976 she entered the National Junior Olympics as a young teenager. She won the pentathlon: the 80-meter high hurdles, 800-meter run, long jump, high jump, and shot put. Her combined scores from the five events made her the winner. She won the event 4 years in a row.

Like many natural athletes, she excelled in other sports, too. Jackie was so proficient at basketball in high school, she earned an athletic scholarship to UCLA, the University of California at Los Angeles. She also got permission to go out for track and field events. There Jackie trained with Bob Kersee, one of the coaches, whom she later married. He encouraged her to prepare for the heptathlon. This seven-event track and field competition is performed over a two-day period. On the first day, the athletes do the 100-meter hurdles, high jump, shot put, and 200-meter dash. On the second day, they do the long jump, javelin throw, and 800-meter run. The training is rigorous and time-consuming because each event requires special training.

While at UCLA, Jackie was diagnosed with asthma. This disease causes chest constriction, coughing, and difficult breathing. Since Jackie was preparing to enter the Olympics, she could not take certain drugs to relieve her asthma because they were banned by the Olympic committee.

Nevertheless, in basketball Jackie was named UCLA's Most Valuable Player. At the 1988 Olympics she won the pentathlon and in 1992 she won the heptathlon.

Reading

1. Jackie called the motto she followed "the three Ds": determination, dedication, and desire. Choose an athletic area in which you wish to succeed. Rank yourself, on a scale of 1 to 10, in the areas of determination, dedication, and desire. Talk with a parent or guardian about your rankings and what you need to do to improve.

2. Jackie had her mother, brother, and coaches to guide her in the decisions she had to make. Who do you turn to for help in making decisions that affect you? Write that person a note of thanks for being there when you need him or her.

3. One of Jackie's role models was Babe Zaharias. Read biographies and books about both and compare and contrast their lives. Share what you learned with your classmates.

4. Jackie is quoted as saying, "I want to be a good statement of the possibilities." In 25 words or less, write what you think she meant in this quote. Share with a classmate what you wrote.

Social Studies

1. Jackie is now a successful businesswoman and has created the Jackie Joyner-Kersee Community Foundation to help inner-city children in East St. Louis, Illinois. Find the city on a map. What direction is it from where you live?

2. At 12, Jackie jumped nearly 17 feet in the long jump competition. Measure 17 feet on your lawn or school yard. How well do you think you could do in comparison? (Jackie jumped into sand on a regulation track. Do not try to do this on hard ground or asphalt. Do it only under supervision of an adult physical education instructor.)

3. Through your teacher, ask a track and field coach to come to your classroom to speak. Prepare questions for him or her on how best to train for certain athletic events. Give the questions to the coach several days in advance.

Further Reading

Green, Carl R. *Jackie Joyner-Kersee.* New York: Crestwood House, 1994.

Harrington, Geri. *Jackie Joyner-Kersee: Champion Athlete.* New York: Chelsea House Publishers, 1995.

Kent, Zachary. *U.S. Olympians.* Chicago, IL: Childrens Press, 1992.

The Lincoln Library of Sports Champions. Volume 7. Columbus, OH: Frontier Press Company, 1993.

Rambeck, Richard. *Jackie Joyner-Kersee.* New York: The Child's World, 1997.

Savage, Jeff. *Running.* Parsippany, NJ: Crestwood House, 1995.

Wickham, Martha. *Superstars of Women's Track and Field.* New York: Chelsea House Publishers, 1997.

Woolum, Janet. *Outstanding Women Athletes: Who They Are and How They Influenced Sports in America.* Phoenix, AZ: The Oryx Press, 1992.

Wright, Gary. *Track & Field: A Step-By-Step Guide.* Mahwah, NJ: Troll Associates, 1990.

Jean-Claude loved to ski. He started at the age of three when the family left St. Cloud, a suburb of Paris, France. They moved to Val d'Isère, a ski resort town in the French Alps, where he skied for hours at a time. After Jean-Claude started school, he took his skis with him and skied during his lunch break. When he and his friends skipped their religion class to ski, the priest donned skis and went after them.

When he was eight, Jean-Claude began winning races. By the age of 10, he was winning against young people who were 13 and 14 years old. But life was not always a pleasant ski run down a mountain- side, for Jean-Claude's parents divorced and sent him to a boarding school some distance from his beloved mountains. There he became withdrawn and sickly. One time he left school to race, but gave no notice where he was going and broke his leg. On his return, the school expelled him.

At 16, Jean-Claude dropped out of school to devote himself to full-time skiing. He carefully watched outstanding skiers handle themselves on the slopes. From his observations, he developed his own style. A broken ankle and serious illnesses, such as amebic dysentery, plagued him. During a term of duty in the French army, he contracted jaundice.

Jean-Claude loved to travel. In 1966 he won the World Championships in Portillo, Chile, for skiing. In the following year, he won races in Austria, France, and Italy. In the United States, he won in the White Mountains of New Hampshire and in Vail, Colorado. When asked why he was so successful, he said he trained hard and kept his thoughts only on skiing. He attained speeds of 80 miles per hour. Before a race, he mentally thought through each turn and twist of the course.

Grenoble, France was host to the 1968 Winter Olympics. The president of France, General Charles de Gaulle, attended. Only once had anyone won three gold medals in skiing. The pressure was on Jean-Claude. Just before the downhill race, one of Jean-Claude's skis lost its wax on some rough ice. There was no time to rewax the ski. Even so, he won by .08 of a second for his first gold medal. He won two more races, one in the fog, for a total of three gold medals! Then he retired from competition.

Jean-Claude's life changed. His hard training was over. He endorsed magazines, clothing, airlines, automobiles, and more. He starred in a movie and a television show. But 4 years later, he knew he must return to skiing. He came out of retirement and became a professional skier. The experts said it was impossible for him to regain his form after such a lengthy time away from skiing, but he worked hard and became the top professional skier in 1972.

Jean-Claude retired again and married Danièle Gauber, a former movie actress. They had three children. Jean-Claude Killy, now a successful businessman, finds his danger in skydiving, bullfighting, and motorbike racing.

Reading

1. In addition to downhill skiing, Jean-Claude enjoyed skydiving, bullfighting, and motorbike racing. Write a paragraph that compares these activities, and explain what you think attracted Jean-Claude to these sports.
2. Choose a classmate for a writing companion. Each of you write a sentence telling what you liked about Jean-Claude Killy. Exchange your sentences and write comments telling your classmate why you agree or disagree with him or her.
3. Draw a picture of Jean-Claude traveling 80 miles per hour down a ski slope.
4. Write a poem—rhymed or unrhymed—about Jean-Claude Killy. Share it with your classmates.

Social Studies

1. Jean-Claude traveled to many places to ski: Chile, Austria, Italy, and the United States (New Hampshire and Colorado). Find these countries and states on a map or globe. Read about them in a reference book. Which one would be your first choice to visit? List the locations in order of your preferences. Explain why you placed them in the order you did.
2. On a physical map of France, find the cities of Paris and Grenoble. Which is located on flat terrain and which is in mountainous terrain?
3. With a classmate, research amebic dysentery and jaundice in a reference book. Discuss with each other the seriousness of each of these diseases.
4. President Charles de Gaulle was a famous French General in World War II. Learn five important things about him from a juvenile biography or reference book. With a panel of two others, in front of your class, discuss your findings.

Further Reading

Aaseng, Nate. Great *Winter Olympic Moments.* Minneapolis, MN: Lerner Publications, 1990.

Arnold, Caroline. *The Olympic Winter Games.* New York: Franklin Watts, 1991.

Brodman, Jonathon, editor. *Athletes.* Volume 2. Danbury, CT: Grolier, 1996.

Dieterich, Michelle. *Skiing: All Action.* Minneapolis, MN: Lerner Publications, 1991.

Gaff, Jackie and David Jefferis. *Skiing and Snow Sports.* New York: Warwick Press, 1990.

Hahn, James and Lynn. *Killy! The Sports Career of Jean-Claude Killy.* Mankato, MN: Crestwood House, 1981.

The Lincoln Library of Sports Champions. Volume 7. Columbus, OH: Frontier Press Company, 1993.

Marozzi, Alfred. *Skiing Basics.* Englewood Cliffs, NJ. Prentice- Hall, 1980.

Sheahan, Casey. *Sports Illustrated Cross-Country Skiing.* New York: Harper & Row, 1984.

Sullivan, George. *Great Lives: Sports.* New York: Charles Scribner's Sons, 1988.

Billie Jean King 1943 • Tennis

Born during World War II, Billie Jean was named for her father, Bill Moffitt, who was in the military service. Hers was a family of sports enthusiasts: Her father enjoyed basketball, her mother was a fine swimmer, and her younger brother became a major league pitcher.

By age 10, Billie Jean became a star as shortstop on a girl's softball team. But she began to realize that there were not many choices for a girl who wanted to excel in sports. Her father suggested that she try tennis. Billie Jean saved her money and bought an $8 tennis racket. She took lessons, practiced hitting a tennis ball against a backyard fence, and found her sport.

One day her pastor, Reverend Bob Richards, an Olympic gold-medal pole vaulter, asked her what she planned to do with her life. "Reverend," Billie responded, "I'm going to be the best tennis player in the world."

Billie Jean worked at becoming the best in tennis. She walked three miles to school to strengthen her legs. By the time she was 16, she ranked nineteenth in the United States. Tennis great Alice Marble gave her lessons, and she jumped to a number-four ranking. Then she married a law student, Larry King, who encouraged her to continue with tennis. She won many tournaments at Wimbledon, England, in women's doubles, singles, and mixed doubles.

In 1968 she turned professional, and by 1971, Billie Jean was the first woman to earn more than $100,000 in tennis. The contrast between earnings for men and for women was great. The top male players that year won nearly three times as much as women did. She became the first woman to win tennis titles on four kinds of tennis surfaces: grass, clay, concrete, and indoor courts.

Because women tennis players were discriminated against in many ways, especially financially, Billie Jean felt she must do something to cause a positive change in attitude among promoters and the public. In 1973 Bobby Riggs, a former 1939 Wimbledon champion, challenged her to a tennis match—man against woman. Bobby, who was 55 years old, was known as a "hustler." He would challenge other players to beat him while he held a suitcase in his hand or wore high heels—and he would win.

Billie Jean accepted the challenge from this man who was 26 years older than she. A promotor and television network put up $400,000 to finance the event. More than 30,000 people came to the Houston Astrodome to watch. Television carried the tennis match to 36 countries around the world.

Billie Jean prepared by studying tapes of Bobby Riggs' playing style so she would not be distracted by his antics. In the match, he soon began to tire. She beat him soundly.

That year she became the first president of the Women's Tennis Association, promoting equal rights for women in athletics. She was one of four athletes in *Life* magazine's list of the "100 Most Important Americans of the Twentieth Century."

Reading

1. Billie Jean often talked aloud to herself as she played tennis. What do you suppose she said?

2. Write a dialogue between Billie Jean and any another athlete you respect. What would they say to each other? On what would they agree and disagree?

3. In what ways is Billie Jean King like someone you know? Make a list and discuss it in class.

4. The top pro athletes now make millions of dollars by using their physical abilities and by endorsing products. Write a short essay on the disadvantages of receiving so much money.

Social Studies

1. *Life* magazine's other three athletes named "most important Americans," were Babe Ruth, Jackie Robinson, and Muhammad Ali. Make a list of five persons, other than athletes, who did the most for humanity during the twentieth dentury. Compare and discuss your list with those of your classmates.

2. If you were asked what you intended to do with your life, what would you answer? Write your answer and discuss it with family or friends.

3. Billie Jean King believed that the men and women who participated in pro tennis tours should be paid equally. In what areas in present-day life are there inequalities between men and women? What do you think should be done? How would you propose doing it?

4. Imagine yourself as a famous tennis player in the year 2020. How old would you be? In what country and location would you be playing? Find the place on a map or globe. Compare your answer to these questions with those of your classmates.

Further Reading

Aaseng, Nathan. *Winning Women of Tennis.* Minneapolis, MN: Lerner Publications, 1981.

Hahn, James and Lynn Hahn. *King! The Sports Career of Billie Jean King.* Mankato, MN: Crestwood House, 1981.

Jones, Betty Millsaps. *Wonder Women of Sports.* New York: Random House, 1981.

The Lincoln Library of Sports Champions. Volume 10. Columbus, OH: Frontier Press Company, 1993.

Lindop, Laurie. *Athletes.* New York: Henry Holt and Company, 1996.

McMane, Fred and Cathrine Wolf. *Winning Women*. New York: Bantam Books, 1995.

Schwabacher, Martin. *Superstars of Women's Tennis.* New York: Chelsea House Publishers, 1997.

Stanford, William R. and Carl R. Green. *Billie Jean King*. New York: Crestwood House, 1993.

______. *Great Lives: Sports.* New York: Charles Scribner's Sons, 1988.

Woolum, Janet. *Outstanding Women Athletes: Who They Are and How They Influenced Sports in America.* Phoenix, AZ: The Oryx Press, 1992.

Olga was very small for her age. Children teased her and asked her when she was going to grow up, but Olga was determined to be an athlete. Her balance was excellent. She could run faster than most. Soon Olga was noticed by adults. By the time she was 11, she was enrolled in a special gymnastic schools in Grodno, in what is now Belarus (Belorussia), near Poland and Lithuania.

Her coach, Renald Ivanovich Knysh, head of the Grodno Sports School, was famous for training Soviet gymnasts. He taught her many new techniques. She was eager to try them. One of the most difficult was the backward somersault on the balance beam. What made it dangerous was landing perfectly, after a back flip, onto a narrow 4½-inch board a few feet off the floor. Olga could not be off-center when she landed or she would take a bad fall. She mastered it after a great deal of practice!

And practice she did: 6 hours a day every day of the week except Sunday. She also had her schoolwork to do. Often she thought of what her mother had taught her: "Be careful, be first, and be joyful." Olga was joyful. Her joy was gymnastics.

The 1972 Olympic Games were held in Munich, West Germany. Eighty-five-pound Olga, at 17, prepared routines for the vault, uneven parallel bars, balance beam, and floor exercise. Seven days before the Olympics, she insisted on a change in the music for her floor exercise. "The Flight of the Bumble Bee" wasn't right for her, for a nasty bee was foreign to her nature, she said. Her coaches stayed up all night devising her gymnastic moves to new music, certain she would not be prepared in time to win a medal.

In the team competition, Olga did well on the vault and the balance beam with her famous back somersault. The crowd cheered. But the uneven bars were a problem, for she slipped and fell. The half-billion people around the world watching on television felt for the gymnast as she finished her routine and left crying in disappointment.

The next day, under tremendous pressure, she performed in the individual apparatus competition. Olga came back and won a silver medal on the uneven parallel bars, a gold for the balance beam, and a gold for the floor exercise with new music! Olga's performance as a gymnast electrified girls around the world. Thousands all over the United States wanted classes in gymnastics.

The Soviet team toured the United States the following year. Wherever they performed, tickets were sold out. Everyone wanted to see Olga. Her fan clubs sprang up all over the country. After winning another silver medal in the 1976 Olympics, Olga retired and became a coach. Later she married Leonid, a musician, and had a son. They came to the United States, where Olga continued to coach gymnastics.

Reading

1. What character trait in Olga Korbut is one that would be good for you to develop over the next few years? Why? Discuss this with your classmates.
2. Olga once said, "If there had not been such a thing as gymnastics, I would have had to invent it." Write sentences telling what that statement means to you. Compare your interpretation with that of a friend.
3. Olga insisted on a change in music because "The Flight of the Bumblebee" did not reflect her personality. What song or type of music best reflects your personality or attitudes? Write a paragraph describing the music and why it suits you.
4. In 30 words or less, write the first paragraph of a news article about Olga Korbut, answering the five Ws (who, what, when, where, why) and How.

Social Studies

1. Olga adopted her mother's philosophy as her own: "Be careful, be first, be joyful." Create a three-part philosophy of your own and compare it with those of your classmates.
2. What is the capital of Belarus (Belorussia)? What direction is it from Grodno?
3. Choose one paragraph from the biography of Olga Korbut. Read it very slowly, thinking about each word as you read. What surprised you when you read it this way?
4. The Olga Korbut Foundation was founded by Olga after the disastrous nuclear power plant accident in Chernobyl in the Ukraine in 1986. Read about the accident in a reference book and find Chernobyl on a map of Ukraine. It is near the capital, Kiev.

Further Reading

Berke, Art. *Gymnastics.* New York: Franklin Watts, 1988.

Bragg, Linda Wallenberg. *Fundamental Gymnastics*. Minneapolis, MN: Lerner Publications, 1995.

Brodman, Jonathon, editor. *Athletes.* Volume 2. Danbury, CT: Grolier, 1996.

Coffey, Wayne. *Olga Korbut.* Woodbridge, CT: Blackbirch Press, 1992.

Cohen, Joel H. *Superstars of Women's Gymnastics.* Philadelphia, PA: Chelsea House Publishers, 1997.

Evans, Gwen. *Eastern Superstar: Olga Korbut.* Milwaukee, WI: Raintree Editions, 1976.

Haycock, Kate. *Gymnastics.* New York: Crestwood House, 1991.

Jensen, Julie. *Beginning Gymnastics.* Minneapolis, MN: Lerner Publications, 1995.

The Lincoln Library of Sports Champions. Volume 10. Columbus, OH: Frontier Press Company, 1993.

Murdock, Tony and Nik Stuart. *Gymnastics.* New York: Franklin Watts, 1989.

Smith, Jay H. *Olga Korbut*. Mankato, MN: Creative Education, 1974.

Little Julie's first ride was on her father's back. Then she rode Twiggy, the family dog. Finally, she rode Dixie, the Shetland pony. The Krones moved to a 10-acre farm in Eau Claire, Michigan. Julie and her older brother had all kinds of pets, especially horses. Mrs. Krone raised horses for sale. One day Julie brought one of the horses into the house. She was having trouble getting the saddle onto the animal. With her mother's help, they devised a pulley over a tree limb to place the saddle on the horse's back.

School wasn't one of Julie's favorite things to do. She preferred riding horses to most anything else. At 17, she dropped out of school to work full time around horses. Her mother took her to Tampa, Florida, to live with her grandparents near the Tampa Bay Downs racetrack.

She got a job as a workout rider exercising thoroughbred race horses. One of the trainers let her ride a horse in one of the races. She did well and soon won five races. That allowed her to be an apprentice rider for one year.

After one race, Julie went up to the track office to talk with another Julie—Julie Snellings. Julie Snellings watched the races on the track's closed circuit TV. She had been a jockey but became paralyzed when a horse fell on her. Now in a wheelchair, she worked in the office and gave good advice to Julie about riding. They became good friends.

Julie worked hard as a jockey. Some male jockeys were not happy to have her riding, nor were some of the fans. Because she was a girl, they thought she should be doing "girl" things. A 100-pound girl controlling an animal weighing more than 1,000 pounds is not easy. But Julie would not give up.

Soon she was winning at racetracks in Florida, Maryland, Delaware, and Pennsylvania. Then she went to the next level of racing where the purses for winning were higher: New Jersey and New York. But there were difficulties along the way. She had serious injuries from spills and falls during the races: a torn muscle in an arm, a concussion, fractures in her arm and ankle, a bruised heart when she fell and a horse stepped on her, and a broken finger. Nevertheless, she got right back up after she healed and began racing again.

Often she was up in the early morning working out with horses, racing them at a track in the afternoon, and racing again in the evening from 7:30 to midnight at another track. On March 6, 1988, she had her 1,205th win. At 24 years old, she was the female jockey with the most wins, but she wanted to be known as a winning jockey, not a winning female jockey.

A high point in her career was the Belmont Stakes. No female jockey had ever won the race. In 1993 Julie won it. By 1994, Julie was the all-time top female jockey, with 2,861 wins. Now people thought of her as a jockey first, who happened to be a woman.

Reading

1. What places or smells does the biography of Julie Krone remind you of ? Make a list and compare it with those of your classmates.
2. After reading biographies of Mario Andretti and Julie Krone, make lists of ways racing cars and racing horses are alike and different. Decide which of the two you prefer.
3. Look through the section on horses in an encyclopedia. Which kind of horse would you prefer to have? Explain to your classmates why you chose the one you did.

Social Studies

1. Read about horse racing in a juvenile book or reference book. Choose three things from your reading that you learned for the first time. Share these with two classmates.
2. Almost everyone has had a particular year that was significant or special to him or her in some way. What year in your life stands out above all the others? Why?
3. The Triple Crown of thoroughbred racing is the Kentucky Derby (Louisville, Kentucky); the Preakness (Baltimore, Maryland); and the Belmont Stakes (Belmont, New York). Find these cities on a map or globe. What are the names of the racetracks where these races are run?
4. Have you ever been discouraged from attempting or doing something because of your sex? Describe what it felt like and how you responded.

Further Reading

Brodman, Jonathon, editor. *Athletes.* Volume 2. Danbury, CT: Grolier Educational Corporation, 1996.

Callahan, Dorothy. *Julie Krone: A Winning Jockey.* Minneapolis MI: Dillon Press, 1990.

Forbis, Judith E. *Hoofbeats Along the Tigris.* Mena, AR: Ansata Publications, 1990.

Gutman, Bill. *Julie Krone*. Austin, TX: Raintree Steck-Vaughn Publishers, 1996.

Harris, Jack C. *The Kentucky Derby.* Mankato, MN: Creative Education, 1990.

Johnson, Neil. *Born to Run: A Racehorse Grows Up.* New York: Scholastic, 1988.

Lindop, Laurie. *Athletes.* New York: Henry Holt and Company, 1996.

McFarland, Cynthia. *Hoofbeats: The Story of a Thoroughbred.* New York: Atheneum, 1993.

McMane, Fred and Cathrine Wolf. *Winning Women.* New York: Bantam Books, 1995.

Spence, Jim. *Julie Krone: Fearless Jockey.* Vero Beach, FL: The Rourke Press, 1995.

Stone, Lynn M. *Bluegrass Country.* Vero Beach, FL: Rourke Corporation, 1993.

William McKinley Lewis, Jr., was the first in his family to attend college. He went to Tuskegee Institute in Alabama, where he played football and was a sprinter on the track team. There he met Evelyn Lawler, who was there on an athletic track and field scholarship. Her areas were the long jump, high jump, and sprint. Evelyn's goal was to be a physical education teacher. After they married, they had three boys and a girl. All the children were athletic, but Carl, their third son, thought of himself as the runt, for even his sister, Carol, who was 2 years younger than Carl, was better than he in many athletic areas.

When Carl was two years old, the family moved to Willingboro, New Jersey. Because there was no track program there, the Lewises created the Willingboro Track Club for the local children. The Lewises took Carl and his sister, Carol, to the practices because they had no money for babysitters. The two children played in a sand pile close by while their parents coached the club members. Carol tried jumping in the sand like those she saw practicing with her parents. Carl just played. At a meet sometime later, they met the famous Jesse Owens, who had won gold medals at the 1936 Olympic Games in Germany. Carl remembered that Jesse told him to "have fun." Now Carl was ready to long jump into sand rather than make castles.

By the time Carl got to high school, he had outgrown his "runt" status. He chose the number 25 for his jacket, because his goal was to jump a record 25 feet before completing high school. He did that and more: At a meet in Memphis, Tennessee, he jumped 25 feet 9 inches. When they met a second time, Jesse Owens had heard about Carl. Soon the media were making comparisons of the two and wondering, in print, if Carl would surpass Jesse's records.

Carl chose the University of Houston for his college education. The track coach, Tom Tellez, was one of the country's most knowledgeable men in track. He helped Carl change his form in the long jump so he wouldn't injure his legs. Coach Tellez had Carl rest several months from long jumping and practice sprinting instead. When the 1984 Olympics began in Los Angeles, California, Carl was ready, but by then, Jesse Owens had died.

Carl won four gold medals in Los Angeles: in the 100 meters, the 200 meters, the long jump, and as a member of the 400-meter relay race. This was the same number of gold medals Jesse had won in 1936.

Four years later, in the 1988 Olympics in Seoul, South Korea, Carl distinguished himself by winning gold medals in the 100 meters and the long jump. He was the first person to ever repeat the feat in the Olympics. His time in the 100 meters was a record 9.86 seconds. In 1992, at the Barcelona, Spain, Olympics, Carl won gold medals in the long jump and the 400-meter relay. There was no other runner or jumper in the world who was able to dominate world-class competition for as many years as Carl did.

Reading

1. Why do you suppose Jesse Owens encouraged Carl to "have fun" when competing in track and field, rather than telling him to win the most events? Discuss your thoughts with your friends and parents.
2. Discuss, with your parents or relatives, who the athletes were in your family. Make a list of sports in which they participated. Select a biography of an athlete you admire whom you think would interest one of these family members, and read it aloud to them.
3. What number would you choose to wear if you set a sports goal to reach in high school? Explain your choice to your classmates.
4. With a teacher, coach, or physical education instructor, discuss what a person must do to promote his or her health as an athlete for a number of years. Make a list of their suggestions. Discuss the list with your classmates.

Social Studies

1. Carl Lewis won Olympic gold medals in the following cities: Los Angeles, California; Seoul, South Korea; and Barcelona, Spain. Locate these cities on a map and read about them in a reference book. With your classmates, discuss several facts you learned about each city.
2. Attend a track meet and take a pad and pencil. Make a list of the events you watch. After each event, rate it from 1 to 10 (1 for least enjoyed; 10 for most enjoyed). Later, discuss your reactions with your classmates or other interested persons.
3. Compare and contrast the lives of Jesse Owens and Carl Lewis in terms of their childhoods and athletic experiences.
4. Talk to some older adults about their memories of people who participated in track and field events. Question them about the athletes and where they observed them competing. Share what you learned with your friends.

Further Reading

Coffey, Wayne. *Carl Lewis.* Woodbridge, CT: Blackbirch Press, 1993.

The Lincoln Library of Sports Champions. Volume 8. Columbus, OH: Frontier Press Company, 1993.

Merrison, Tim. *Field Athletics*. New York: Crestwood House, 1991.

Osborn, Kevin. *Scholastic Encyclopedia of Sports in the United States.* New York: Scholastic, 1997.

Rosenthal, Bert. *Track and Field.* Austin, TX: Raintree Steck-Vaughn, 1994.

Sandelson, Robert. *Track Athletics.* New York: Crestwood House, 1991.

Savage, Jeff. *Running*. Parsippany, NJ: Crestwood House, 1995.

Wright, Gary. *Track & Field: A Step-By-Step Guide.* Mahwah, NJ: Troll Associates, 1990.

Nancy Lopez

1957 • Golf

Nancy Lopez's father, Domingo, dropped out of school when he was in the third grade. Domingo had to help his family earn a living so they could eat. They had just moved from Mexico to the United States. He worked hard in the fields. Later, he met Marina and they were married. After serving in the U.S. Army, he learned to repair cars. The owner of the shop where Domingo worked taught him to play golf and he excelled quickly.

Marina developed a lung disease and the doctor prescribed walking to help her regain her health. She and Domingo walked together on the public golf links of Roswell, New Mexico. When Nancy, their second daughter, could walk, she followed them around the golf course on weekends, so they did not need a babysitter. By now, Domingo owned and operated the auto-body shop.

One day, when Nancy was 8 years old, Domingo handed her one of her mother's clubs and said to keep hitting the golf ball until it went into a hole. And hit it she did, right over their heads. Domingo became her golf teacher. By the age of nine, she won her first tournament by 110 strokes!

Marina sacrificed by giving up golf so there would be money for Nancy to play on the public golf links. Because of discrimination against Mexican Americans, they could not play on some of the better golf courses. Domingo worked extra hours and put aside $100 a month to help Nancy travel to tournaments.

By the time Nancy was 12 years old, she won the New Mexico State Women's Amateur Championship. Domingo built an addition to their house to show the trophies he was sure she would win. Nancy played on the all-male high school golf team. She later got an athletic scholarship to play at the University of Tulsa in Oklahoma.

After 2 years in college, Nancy dropped out to become a professional golfer. She wanted to pay back her parents for all the sacrifices they had made for her. She joined the Ladies Professional Golf Association (LPGA) tour in 1977 when she was 20. Misfortune hit the family that year when Marina died after surgery for a ruptured appendix. Nancy remembered her mother telling her to practice hard, work hard, and be number one. In 1978 Nancy won five tournaments in a row! She was named Rookie of the Year and Player of the Year, the first person to receive both honors in one year.

People began following her on the golf tour and called themselves "Nancy's Navy," much like those who called themselves "Arnie's Army," after the famous male golf star, Arnold Palmer.

Nancy continued to win many victories on the pro tour. By 1985 her average score for a game was a fabulous 71.73. In 1982 she married Ray Knight, a major-league baseball player and coach, and they had three children. Nancy was inducted into the LPGA Hall of Fame at the age of 30 and won her third LPGA championship in 1989.

Reading

1. Read about the game of golf in a reference book. Define the following terms: par, birdie, bogey, eagle, and ace.
2. The word *Domingo* is a Spanish word for a day in the week. Nancy's father was sometimes called the English translation of this word. What is the translation? What are the days of the week in Spanish?
3. If you were asked to write about the most important event in the biography of Nancy Lopez, what would be your focus? Why?
4. What three things do you think made Nancy Lopez so successful as a golfer? Put them in order of importance. Discuss your thoughts with your classmates. Do they agree? Why or why not?

Social Studies

1. In what section of New Mexico is the city of Roswell located?
2. Read about the state of New Mexico in a reference book. Report to your classmates five interesting facts that you found about the state.
3. Make a list of five sacrifices you would make if you had a child who showed the possibility of becoming an exceptional athlete. Compare your list with those of your classmates.
4. What are some reasons a very good athlete should continue in college and complete his or her degree program before turning professional? Discuss with your classmates.

Further Reading

Hahn, James and Lynn Hahn. *Nancy Lopez, Golfing Pioneer.* St. Paul, MN: EMC Corporation, 1979.

Jensen, Julie. *Beginning Golf.* Minneapolis, MN: Lerner Publications, 1995.

Krause, Peter. *Fundamental Golf.* Minneapolis, MN: Lerner Publications, 1995.

The Lincoln Library of Sports Champions. Volume 11. Columbus, OH: Frontier Press Company, 1993.

Lindop, Laurie. *Athletes.* New York: Henry Holt and Company, 1996.

Phillips, Betty Lou. *The Picture Story of Nancy Lopez.* New York: Julian Messner, 1980.

Robison, Nancy. Nancy Lopez: *Wonder Woman of Golf.* Chicago, IL: Childrens Press, 1979.

Schumacher, Craig. *Nancy Lopez*. Mankato, MN: Creative Education Society, 1979.

Wilner, Barry. *Superstars of Women's Golf.* Philadelphia: Chelsea House Publishers, 1997.

Woolum, Janet. *Outstanding Women Athletes: Who They Are and How They Influenced Sports in America.* Phoenix, AZ: The Oryx Press, 1992.

Joe was born in Alabama to Munroe and Lillie Barrow. They had eight children. Munroe was a sharecropper on a 120-acre farm. Because of mental illness, Munroe was placed in an institution, where he later died. Lillie later married a widower with eight children of his own. The family of eighteen moved to Detroit to find work. Then the Great Depression hit the world.

In 1931 Joe was 17 years old and 6 feet tall. Embarrassed, he hid a rented violin under his coat. With a hard-earned 50 cents in change from his mother, Joe went to his violin lesson. But a friend talked him into going to a gym where boxers trained. There he learned that he could fight as an amateur for merchandise checks for up to $25. His violin teacher contacted Lillie, and they decided boxing was a better career choice for Joe. So during the day he delivered ice (there were no refrigerators then) or worked in an auto factory. He trained at the gym in the evenings.

Joe fought under the name of Joe Louis. His potential as a boxer was soon known. John Roxborough, a real estate agent and gambler, sought Joe out, became his manager, and hired Jack Blackburn as his trainer. The deal was that when Joe turned pro, he would split his winnings 50/50 with Roxborough. Until that time, Roxborough would keep him in spending money, clothes, and equipment, and take charge of his training and fight schedule.

Joe's first pro fight in 1934 lasted less than 2 minutes. Blackburn trained Joe to go for a knockout every time because African American fighters generally lost decisions against white opponents. Secondly, he said, "Kill the body and the head will die!" That's what Joe did in his first pro fight: he beat on the man's ribs until the fighter lowered his guard. A swift left hook to the chin ended the fight.

Joe could not forget his fight against Max Schmeling, a German. That was his first pro defeat. It ended in the twelfth round on June 19, 1936. Joe felt humiliated. The rematch was set for June 22, 1938. Adolph Hitler was beginning World War II and wanted Max to beat Joe again to show that Germans were a master race. Joe was under pressure too. President Roosevelt told him the country was depending on his muscles for America.

Joe was ready. He beat Max in 2 minutes and 4 seconds. He knocked Max down three times. Max spent 2 weeks in the hospital before returning home to Germany. Later, after the war, Max and Joe became friends.

In 1942 Joe volunteered to go into the army. He appeared in a movie, *This Is the Army*, and toured military bases, giving boxing exhibitions. During his 4 years in the service, he fought in 96 exhibitions and visited countless GIs everywhere.

Joe Louis, who was nicknamed the "Brown Bomber," became the heavyweight champion of the world in 1937 by defeating Jim Braddock. He reigned for 11 years as the champion, the longest any heavyweight ever held the title.

Reading

1. Write a poem (rhyming or non-rhyming) about why boxing is a career for you, or why it should be discontinued as a sport. Share your poem with your classmates.
2. Look up *sharecropper* in a dictionary or reference book. What does it mean?
3. Choose any incident in Joe Louis's biography and make it into a cartoon. Give your drawing a caption.
4. Pretend Joe Louis asked you to come to the gym to watch him train. What three questions would you ask him when he took a break? Write them down and compare them with those of your classmates.

Social Studies

1. Joe Louis won more than $4,000,000 as a fighter but spent or gave most of it away. What advice would you have given Joe if he had asked you? Be specific.
2. Joe thought Max Schmeling would be a "pushover" in their first fight. How would you have consoled Joe after he was beaten the first time? What would you have said to him?
3. To many African Americans at the time, Joe Louis was a hero. Do you have a personal hero or someone you look up to? Write a character description of that person, and explain why he or she is important to you.
4. Read the records of other professional boxers in a reference book. How do they compare to those of Joe Louis?

Further Reading

Fitzgerald, Jim. *Boxing for Beginners.* New York: Atheneum, 1980.

Jakoubek, Robert. *Joe Louis: Heavyweight Champion.* New York: Chelsea House Publishers, 1990.

Knapp, Ron. *Top 10 Heavyweight Boxers.* Springfield, NJ: Enslow Publishers, 1997.

Libby, Bill. *Joe Louis: The Brown Bomber.* New York: Lothrop, Lee & Shepard Books, 1980.

The Lincoln Library of Sports Champions. Volume 11. Columbus, OH: Frontier Press Company, 1993.

Lipsyte, Robert. *Joe Louis: A Champ for All America.* New York: HarperCollinsPublishers, 1994.

Osborn, Kevin. *Scholastic Encyclopedia of Sports in the United States.* New York: Scholastic, 1997.

Ricciuti, Edward R. *How to Box: A Guide for Beginners.* New York: Thomas Y. Crowell, 1982.

Alice Marble

1913-1990 • TENNIS

Alice spent the first 6 years of her life on a farm in northeastern California. Her father thought that farming was too strenuous for his wife, Jessie, so he took a job in San Francisco and moved his wife and five children there. The worldwide flu epidemic of 1919 struck the Marble family that year. Alice's father, who was just getting over injuries from an automobile accident, became ill with the flu and died on Christmas Eve.

With bills to pay, Jessie took a job cleaning offices at 4 o'clock in the morning, and then came home to get the children off to school. Alice's brothers quit school and got jobs to support the family. Jessie's brother introduced Alice to baseball. She loved it and played catch during practice with the local baseball team, the San Francisco Seals. But her brother, Dan, who had assumed the role of head of the house, thought tennis was a more ladylike game for her. He bought her a tennis racket and encouraged her to play. Dan was strict, allowed no dating, and made sure she got to bed early.

Alice was unhappy but did as she was told. In fact, she enjoyed tennis. The more she played, the better she became. Newspapers said she played more like a man than a woman. In 1930 Alice, coached by the highly regarded Eleanor "Teach" Tennant, was ranked third in the country.

In an all-day tournament, playing in 104-degree heat, Alice collapsed. The doctors diagnosed her ailment as sunstroke, anemia, and other physical problems. After hospitalization, Alice worked on both diet and exercise. By 1936, she was winning singles, doubles, and mixed-doubles matches at Wimbledon and in the United States. Alice was named Female Athlete of the Year by the Associated Press in 1939 and 1940.

In the early 1940s, the world was engulfed in World War II, so international tennis tournaments were suspended. Alice met Joe Crowley, an army captain. They were married and looked forward to the end of the war. But on Christmas Eve, 1944, Alice received a telegram from the War Department that Joe had been killed over Germany. Alice was grief-stricken. Several months later, U.S. military intelligence contacted Alice to conduct tennis matches in Switzerland. The true purpose of her mission was to spy on a banker she knew before the war. He lived in Switzerland and was suspected of helping the Nazis smuggle stolen treasures out of Germany. The banker's records were needed to convict the Nazis. Alice got the records but was shot by a double agent as she fled for her life.

After the war, Alice lectured, taught tennis, and wrote a second autobiography. An angry editorial she wrote for *American Lawn Tennis* magazine helped break down the racial barrier that kept Althea Gibson and other African American tennis players from playing in major tennis tournaments.

Reading

1. Alice's life was not always pleasant. List several of her difficult experiences. Which one on your list do you think was the most difficult? Discuss this with your classmates.
2. What is the difference between a singles, a doubles, and a mixed-doubles tennis match? Find the answer in a reference book or ask someone who is familiar with tennis.
3. List five interesting facts about Alice Marble. Compare your list with those of your classmates.
4. Summarize the life of Alice Marble in exactly 30 words. Read your summary aloud to your parents or classmates.

Social Studies

1. Read about World War II in a reference book. Report to your classmates five things of interest to you that happened in one of the following theaters of war: Europe, northern Africa, Asia, or the Pacific. With which side was Switzerland allied during World War II?
2. Alice Marble wrote an editorial that helped break down racial barriers in professional tennis. Choose an issue you feel strongly about. Then write an editorial that explains your position.
3. After Alice had sunstroke while playing tennis too long in the summer, she put a wet cabbage leaf inside her hat, as some farm workers do on hot days. She believed this helped her to stay cool. Talk to your parents or other adults about home remedies that people use. Discuss them with your classmates.
4. Read about anemia in a reference book. Explain what you learn to your classmates.

Further Reading

Coombs, Charles. *Be a Winner in Tennis.* New York: William Morrow and Company, 1975.

MacCurdy, Doug and Shawn Tully. *Sports Illustrated Tennis.* New York: Harper & Row, 1980.

Marble, Alice. *The Road to Wimbledon.* New York: Charles Scribner's Sons, 1946.

Miller, Marc. *Fundamental Tennis.* Minneapolis, MN: Lerner Publications, 1995.

Osborn, Kevin. *Scholastic Encyclopedia of Sports in the United States.* New York: Scholastic, 1997.

Singleton, Skip. *The Junior Tennis Handbook: A Complete Guide to Tennis for Juniors, Parents, and Coaches.* Cincinnati, OH: Shoe Tree Press, 1991.

Sullivan, George. *Better Tennis for Boys and Girls.* New York: Dodd, Mead & Company, 1987.

Robert "Bob" Mathias was born in the town of Tulare in the San Joaquin Valley of California. From his father, a medical doctor, Bob inherited his physique and easy-going nature; from his mother he learned, among other things, how to relax.

Tulare, a small dairy, fruit, and cotton center, was a good place for the Mathias children. Even though Dr. Mathias was often paid by his patients with eggs, milk, fresh fruits, and vegetables during the Great Depression of the 1930s, he was able to build a backyard gymnasium for his four children and those of the neighbors. It included a hurdle, high jump, parallel bars, and shot and discus pit. The public school playgrounds, with all their equipment and space, were just a few minutes away.

Misfortune hit Bob when he was 11. He became sick with anemia, followed by chicken pox, measles, and whooping cough, one after the other. Bob had difficulty sleeping, so his mother taught him to fall asleep by relaxing one body part at a time, beginning with his toes and ending at the top of his head. He would often be asleep by the time he got to his arms. His father prescribed rest, vitamins, and much wholesome food. Bob drank a gallon of milk a day. He got better and stronger.

At 16, Bob began winning track meets. His track coach, Virgil Jackson, recognized Bob as a potential Olympic champion and suggested that he train for the decathlon, a ten-event sport.

Bob had never participated in the javelin throw. In fact, there was no javelin in Tulare, so one was ordered from Los Angeles. With just a few months to prepare, Bob trained diligently. He qualified for the 1948 Olympics at age 17. His goal was to win a third-place bronze medal against his older, more experienced competitors.

That year the Olympics were held in London, England. The 10 decathlon events were held within a 2-day period. Late into the night of the second day, on a cold, rain-soaked field, Bob Mathias became the youngest person to win the Olympic decathlon. Between events, he wrapped himself with a blanket and fell asleep by relaxing as his mother had taught him. By doing this, he conserved his energy and kept his muscles from knotting up. That year Bob was also awarded the James E. Sullivan Memorial Trophy as the best amateur athlete.

Bob went to Stanford and lead the school's football team to its first conference title in 12 years. The 1952 Rose Bowl followed, but Stanford lost to Illinois. That same year, he went to the Olympics in Helsinki, Finland, and won the decathlon again. No Olympic athlete had ever done that!

Hollywood beckoned when Bob returned home. He was cast as himself in *The Bob Mathias Story* and starred in a TV series called "The Trouble Shooters." In 1966 Bob was elected to the U.S. Congress and served for 8 years.

Reading

1. Bob Mathias inherited certain characteristics from his parents. Make a list of some of the characteristics you may have inherited from your parents. Sometimes you can recognize physical characteristics from pictures of parents when they were your age. With your parents, discuss ways in which you think you are alike.
2. In a reference book read about the 10 decathlon events at the Olympics. List, in order of events, those played the first day and the second day. Describe them to your classmates or relatives.
3. Read about Olympic track and field events. Discuss, with classmates, five things that surprised you.
4. Pretend you are permitted to interview Bob Mathias. List five things you would ask him. Compare your list with those of your classmates.

Social Studies

1. Anemia, chicken pox, measles, and whooping cough afflicted eleven-year-old Bob Mathias. With two or three friends, read about these diseases in a reference book. Report on them, as a group, to your classmates.
2. Bob Mathias won Olympic gold medals in the cities of London, England, and Helsinki, Finland. If you flew directly from London to Helsinki, over which European country and which Scandinavian country would you fly?
3. The Central Valley, also called the Great Valley, in California has two main river systems. The San Joaquin is in the south. What is the one in the north? Refer to a physical map of California, if necessary.
4. The Great Depression was the worst and longest business downturn in modern times. Who was president during those years?

Further Reading

Kent, Zachary. *U.S. Olympians.* Chicago, IL: Childrens Press, 1992.

The Lincoln Library of Sports Champions. Volume 12. Columbus, OH: Frontier Press Company, 1993.

Merrison, Tim. *Field Athletics.* New York: Crestwood House, 1991.

Scott, Jim. *Bob Mathias: Champion of Champions.* Englewood Cliffs, NJ: Prentice-Hall, 1952.

Sullivan, George. *Great Lives: Sports.* New York: Charles Scribner's Sons, 1988.

Tassin, Myron. *Bob Mathias: The Life of the Olympic Champion.* New York: St. Martin's Press, 1984.

Wright, Gary. *Track & Field: A Step-By-Step Guide.* Mahwah, NJ: Troll Associates, 1990.

Zarnowski, Frank. *A Basic Guide to Decathlon.* Glendale, CA: Griffin Publishing, 1996.

The surfers off the coast of California enjoyed being with little Pat Keller. They would throw her into the air from their surfboards and she would do somersaults and twists before entering the wave they were riding. Pat liked swimming, but diving was better.

Pat trained at the Los Angeles Aquatic Club. As a teenager, she practiced her diving six days a week by doing 80 to 100 dives a day. In 1947 she came in second at the national competition. A year later, she missed going to the Olympics by one point, but she kept competing and soon had 27 national diving titles to her credit.

Pat married an airline pilot, Glen McCormick. He not only encouraged her to continue diving, he also served as her coach and as the coach of the U.S. diving team. Pat practiced particularly difficult dives. In competition, dives are listed by their degree of difficulty from 0 to 10. The highest mark goes to the diver who does a difficult dive exceptionally well. Pat wanted to be the best.

When the 1952 Olympics came around, Pat was ready to go to Helsinki, Finland. At 22, she had maturity and the experience that her younger teammates did not, as yet, have. Pat helped them, and they came home from Helsinki with five of six medals for diving. Pat was the first female diver in history to win two golds.

Before the next Olympics, Pat won gold medals in the Pan-American Games. Then she became pregnant with her first child. Although she could not dive, she did swim a half mile every day until 2 days before her son, Timothy, was born. That left her with 5 months to get into condition and qualify for the 1956 Olympics in Melbourne, Australia. And qualify she did!

In Melbourne, Pat was ahead by 17 points in the three-meter springboard. Platform diving was another matter. There, she was in fourth place with only one dive left to capture a gold medal. The dive she chose was a forward one-and-a-half somersault with a full twist. That dive secured her the gold medal, one of two she received in the 1956 Olympics. She became the first diver in Olympic history, male or female, to defend gold medals in both platform and springboard diving.

Many awards came Pat's way: The Associated Press's Athlete of the Year (1956) and the Sullivan Award as the country's best amateur athlete of the year. *Sports Illustrated* named her their Woman Athlete of the year. In 1965 Pat was elected to the Swimming Hall of Fame in Fort Lauderdale. To continue her contributions to diving excellence, she organized a diving camp in which young people could learn from her experience.

In the opening ceremonies of the 1984 Olympics, Pat was one of those selected to bring the Olympic flag into the Los Angeles Coliseum. That year Kelly, her daughter, competed. Kelly made her mother proud of her by winning a silver medal in diving.

Reading

1. Pat probably has some memories of surfing and flipping into the ocean waves as a small child. What water experiences do you remember when you were younger? Share them with your classmates.
2. List several character traits that you noticed when reading Pat McCormick's biography. Compare your list with those of your classmates.
3. Wander around a swimming pool with a note pad and pencil. Write down what you see, hear, and feel. Rewrite your notes and read them to your classmates or parents. Make a poem from what you wrote.
4. Draw one picture of a diver diving from a springboard and one diving from a high platform. Also show them as they enter the water. Check a reference book to see how accurate you made your drawings.

Social Studies

1. In a reference book read about Helsinki, Finland, and Melbourne, Australia. Prepare to tell your classmates what you would see if you had the opportunity to visit them.
2. Springboard and platform diving require different kinds of dives. Research these two types of diving forms with a classmate, and prepare a class presentation on what you learned.
3. Imagine having Pat as a friend. Write a scene where you have a pizza or another food you both like. What would you discuss as you ate together?
4. Compare and contrast the lives of Pat McCormick and Gertrude Ederle. In what ways were they alike and in what ways were they different?

Further Reading

Kent, Zachary. *U.S. Olympians.* Chicago, IL: Childrens Press, 1992.

The Lincoln Library of Sports Champions. Volume 11. Columbus, OH: Frontier Press Company, 1993.

Osborn, Kevin. *Scholastic Encyclopedia of Sports in the United States.* New York: Scholastic, 1997.

Sandelson, Robert. *Swimming and Diving.* New York: Crestwood House, 1991.

Verrier, John. *Swimming and Diving.* Crystal Lake, IL: Rigby Education, 1996.

Wilson, Charlie G. *Swimming and Diving.* Morristown, NJ: Silver Burdett Press, 1987.

Woolum, Janet. *Outstanding Women Athletes: Who They Are and How They Influenced Sports in America.* Phoenix, AZ: The Oryx Press, 1992.

Shannon Miller was born with leg problems. Her pediatrician said she must wear braces for a year and do exercises so her feet would not turn inward. Special shoes attached to a metal bar turned her feet in the right direction. Some months later at a shopping mall, Shannon wandered away from her mother. She was found 20 minutes later trying on shoes in the men's shoe department. Even with shoes on, her tiny feet fit right into the men's shoes.

The family moved to Edmond, Oklahoma. Five-year-old Shannon and her 7-year-old sister, Tessa, decided they wanted a trampoline for Christmas. Their parents, Claudia and Ron, were not sure it was the best thing for them, but their grandmother offered to pay for part of it, and so they bought a used one. The two girls jumped and flipped and enjoyed it. But Claudia decided it was too dangerous and offered them gymnastics lessons instead. Shannon found that gymnastics was just what she wanted to do.

When Shannon was eight, the local gymnastics club traveled to the Soviet Union to study the gymnastic program there. The Soviet coaches noted Shannon's potential and encouraged Claudia to find her special training. Claudia and Ron found Steve Nunno coaching 45 minutes away in Oklahoma City. Steve had assisted Bela Karolyi, the former coach of Nadia Comaneci and Mary Lou Retton. Shannon started lessons immediately.

When she was 13, Shannon Miller became a U.S. Olympic team member. Coach Nunno and Peggy Liddick, the U.S. Olympic coach, prepared her for the 1992 Olympic trials. In spite of an injured elbow that required surgery, Shannon recovered quickly and earned a place on the team.

Barcelona, Spain, hosted the summer Olympic Games in 1992. Shannon was the smallest and shortest of all the U.S. athletes participating. She was 4 feet 6 inches tall and weighed 69 pounds. She won two silver and three bronze medals!

Returning to the United States, she stopped off in Washington, D.C., with the other U.S. Olympians and met President George Bush and Arnold Schwarzenegger. When she returned to Edmond, Oklahoma, there was a parade for her and a new car—which she could not drive because she was only 15.

Training did not stop, though. The World Gymnastics Championship in Birmingham, England, was next. She won the world title there by .007 points. This was followed the next year by the World Championships in Brisbane, Australia. Shannon became the first American to win back-to-back World Championships.

Shannon continued in public school during this time, making straight As. She was named to the National Honor Society for 4 years in a row. She also continued to train, and in the 1996 Olympic Games in Atlanta, Georgia, Shannon received a gold medal as a member of the U.S. women's gymnastics team and a gold medal for her individual performance on the balance beam.

Reading

1. A person's size does not always indicate how well he or she may do in the Olympics or in any other competition. List four other characteristics that are often more important than size or strength. Read biographies of other athletes who did not rely on size and strength to become winners.

2. What is the most important word in this biography? Why? What is the most important phrase in this biography? Why? What was the most important city to which Shannon went? Why?

3. Compare and contrast the lives of Nadia Comaneci and Shannon Miller.

4. Using the picture of Shannon Miller in the biography, write a word portrait of her in one hundred words or less.

Social Studies

1. On a map or globe, locate the following places where Shannon competed in gymnastics: Barcelona, Spain; Birmingham, England; Brisbane, Australia; and Atlanta, Georgia.

2. Read about the cities of Barcelona, Birmingham, Brisbane, and Atlanta. Why do you think the Olympic committee chose them as Olympic sites? Which one holds the most interest for you? Share with your classmates three things of interest about the city you chose.

3. Shannon injured her elbow and needed surgery. Discuss with your classmates how an injury might be beneficial to a person.

4. Based on the information in the short biography of Shannon Miller, write another biography of what she might be doing when she is 40 or 50 years old.

Further Reading

Berke, Art. *Gymnastics.* New York: Franklin Watts, 1988.

Bragg, Linda Wallenberg. *Fundamental Gymnastics.* Minneapolis, MN: Lerner Publications, 1995.

Durrant, Amanda. *My Book of Gymnastics: Health & Movement.* New York: Thomson Learning, 1993.

Green, Septima. *Going for the Gold: Shannon Miller.* New York: Avon Books, 1996.

Haycock, Kate. *Gymnastics.* New York: Crestwood House, 1991.

Jackman, Joan. *The Young Gymnast: A Young Enthusiast's Guide to Gymnastics.* New York: Dorling Kindersley, 1995.

Jensen, Julie. *Beginning Gymnastics.* Minneapolis, MN: Lerner Publications, 1995.

McMane, Fred and Cathrine Wolf. *Winning Women.* New York: Bantam Books, 1995.

Quiner, Krista. *Shannon Miller: America's Most Decorated Gymnast: A Biography.* East Hanover, NJ: The Bradford Book Company, 1997.

Tames, Richard. *The Modern Olympics.* Crystal Lake, IL: Rigby Education, 1996.

Martina was born into a family of athletes in Prague, Czechoslovakia. Her grandmother was an excellent tennis player; her mother, Jana, was a skier, and her father was a ski patrolman. Martina's mother and father divorced when she was three. As a child, Martina loved soccer, ice skating, bicycle riding, and ice hockey. She did well in each of these sports.

Jana later married Mirek Navratil. Martina and her mother now had the last name of Navratilova, for in Czechoslovakia wives and daughters add "ova" after the man's family name.

Mirek loved tennis and taught Martina how to play. He planted in her mind the thought of playing at Wimbledon, the famous tennis competition in England. By the time she was eight years old, Martina had won her first tournament.

When she was 11, the Soviet Union, another communist country, suddenly invaded her country. Out of fear, Martina hid in a store for several hours until her father found her. The Communist government of Czechoslovakia gave its people little freedom of choice. Life was difficult. The new family lived in a small apartment without hot water. Mirek rode his motorbike to work. Since Martina had such strength in tennis, the government allowed her travel privileges so the rest of the world could see one of Czechoslovakia's best athletes.

At 16, Martina played in a tennis tournament in Fort Lauderdale, Florida. While there she fell in love with pizza, hamburgers, fried chicken, and pancakes—foods not available in Czechoslovakia. She gained weight, which affected her playing. Her new American friends taught her the importance of diet and exercise, which were necessary if she was to continue playing winning tennis.

One of Martina's favorite subjects in school was geography. She learned to speak three European languages. Because she traveled in the United States, she learned English too. Martina's excellence in tennis took her to many of the countries she studied in geography: Tokyo, Japan; Paris, France; Rome, Italy; London, England; Sydney, Australia; and the United States. When she was 18, she decided to defect while on a tennis tour in the United States. This meant she could not go back to her country to live or even see her parents. She also had to be careful when traveling not to go to a country that would allow the Czechoslovakian authorities to take her back. Most of all, she missed her parents.

Some of the money Martina earned playing tennis was used for buying her parents a home and apple orchard in Czechoslovakia. The government controlled newspapers and would not tell about her many tennis championships. Her telephone bills to her parents were often huge. But in 1979, Jana was finally allowed to travel to see her play at Wimbledon, where her father had predicted she would play. That year her mother saw her win one of several Wimbledon championships.

Reading

1. In a reference book, read about the many tennis championships Martina won throughout the world. Discuss with your friends those you think are most important and why you think so.

2. What advice would you give a person who loved to eat junk food but also wanted to excel in athletics? Make a list of healthy foods a person might eat at each meal on a normal day.

3. Reread the first paragraph of the biography. In order of your preference, list the sports Martina enjoyed as a child. Which one, if any, would be your first choice?

4. Fill in the blank: I enjoyed (or did not enjoy) Martina's biography because ________________.

Social Studies

1. On a world map or globe use your finger to locate a few of the many places Martina went: Tokyo, Japan; Sydney, Australia; Rome, Italy; London, England; and Fort Lauderdale, Florida. In a reference book, find the city you know the least about and search for five things of interest that would make you want to visit there. Share your findings with your friends.

2. The former Czechoslovakia is now two countries. What are their names? In which one is Martina's birthplace located?

3. Which sport do you think is the favorite with the boys and which is the favorite with the girls in your classroom? Write your answer. Now take a survey of your classmates and find out what they say is their favorite. Did you guess correctly?

4. What countries now border the Czech Republic?

Further Reading

Aaseng, Nathan. *Winning Women of Tennis.* Minneapolis, MN: Lerner Publications, 1981.

Coombs, Charles. *Be a Winner in Tennis.* New York: William Morrow and Company, 1975.

Jones, Betty Millsaps. *Wonder Women of Sports.* New York: Random House, 1981.

Knudson, R. R. *Martina Navratilova: Tennis Power.* New York: Viking Kestrel, 1986.

MacCurdy, Doug and Shawn Tully. *Sports Illustrated Tennis.* New York: Harper & Row, 1980.

McMane, Fred and Cathrine Wolf. *Winning Women.* New York: Bantam Books, 1995.

Schwabacher, Martin. *Superstars of Women's Tennis.* New York: Chelsea House Publishers, 1997.

Singleton, Skip. *The Junior Tennis Handbook: A Complete Guide to Tennis for Juniors, Parents, and Coaches.* Cincinnati, OH: Shoe Tree Press, 1991.

Sullivan, George. *Better Tennis for Boys and Girls.* New York: Dodd, Mead & Company, 1987.

________. *Great Lives: Sports.* New York: Charles Scribner's Sons, 1988.

Woolum, Janet. *Outstanding Women Athletes: Who They Are and How They Influenced Sports in America.* Phoenix, AZ: The Oryx Press, 1992.

Jesse Owens

1913-1980 • Track and Field

Every winter, as a child, James Cleveland (J. C.) Owens had pneumonia. The Oakville, Alabama, house the family lived in as sharecroppers was drafty, with no running water or bathroom, and only a fireplace for heating and cooking. Mrs. Owens wrapped J. C. in cotton sacks to sweat out the illnesses he caught. When he was six years old, he not only had pneumonia, but he had a bump on his leg that got larger and hurt him when he walked.

There was no doctor available, so his mother heated a knife and his father and an older brother held him down while she cut open the lump. Fortunately, the operation was successful and he could walk and run again.

One of his sisters moved to Cleveland, Ohio, and wrote back to the family that there was work for black people in that city. The mule was sold and the money spent on a train ticket for the family to move. They found an apartment with running water and an indoor bathroom. In Cleveland there were parks, stores, the lake, and even a large brick school with many classrooms.

Now J. C. could go to school all year long and not have to drop out to help on the farm in the spring. The first day of school, he was asked his name. J. C.'s southern drawl was difficult for the teacher to understand. She thought she heard "Jesse." He was too nervous to correct her. The name stuck. He liked it and he remained Jesse Owens the rest of his life.

The coach at the school, Charles Riley, watched Jesse as he played. One day he asked Jesse to join the track team after school. Jesse was delighted, but then remembered he had three different jobs to do after school to help support the family. The coach worked with him before school for 45 minutes each day.

By the time Jesse was a senior at East Tech High School, he was voted class president and became the captain of the track team. His high school track record was 75 victories in 79 races.

Coach Riley, whom Jesse affectionately called "Pop," helped Jesse get into Ohio State University. There Jesse worked at three jobs to get through school. On May 25, 1935, he broke five world records and equaled another in just 45 minutes! But other big days awaited Jesse. He qualified for the 1936 Olympics in Berlin, Germany. Adolph Hitler, Germany's dictator, used the Olympics to show off what were called "Hitler's Olympics." He told everyone, especially the Germans, that they were a superior race. Blacks and Jews could never compete with them, he said. But Jesse won four gold medals and set three Olympic records.

Jesse Owens came home to his wife, Ruth Solomon (whom he had met in his early teens), and their three girls. He then settled into the hectic life of speaking engagements and radio shows. He formed his own public relations company. In 1976 President Gerald Ford awarded him the Medal of Freedom, the highest award given to a U.S. citizen.

Reading

1. As a child, Jesse had never been to a city. Think about a city you know and pretend you are Jesse. Write about the things you see when you visit there and how it affects you after living on a farm.

2. When Jesse was operated on by his mother, without an anesthetic to relieve the pain, he later realized he could endure a lot. This experience helped him through other painful experiences in life. Have you had a painful experience that made you a better person? Write in a few sentences how it changed you.

3. Read about the various track and field events in which Jesse Owens set records. All his records have been broken now. Which ones are the most impressive to you? Why? Discuss your opinions with your friends or parents.

4. Jesse held down three jobs so that he could attend college and run track. Think of something important that you would like to do. Describe what it is and explain whether you would work three jobs in order to attain your goal.

Social Studies

1. On which of the Great Lakes is Cleveland located? In a reference book, read about Cleveland and share two interesting facts with your class or friends.

2. Charles Riley, Jesse's first coach, told him, "Never forget this: There's bound to come a time in your life when you'll be asked for more than ability. When that happens, you'll have to make up the difference—in manhood." What does this quote mean to you? Give some examples in which a person might have to go beyond his or her abilities to succeed.

3. How did Jesse Owens's performance in the 1936 Olympics in Berlin, Germany, help expose the falseness of Hitler's racist theories?

4. Write a series of questions you would want Jesse to answer if he were alive. Read them to your classmates and ask them to answer how they think Jesse would answer.

Further Reading

Adler, David A. *A Picture Book of Jesse Owens*. New York: Holiday House, 1992.

Gentry, Tony. *Jesse Owens: Champion Athlete.* New York: Chelsea House Publishers, 1990.

Kent, Zachary. *U.S. Olympians.* Chicago, IL: Childrens Press, 1992.

Krull, Kathleen. *Lives of the Athletes: Thrills, Spills (and What the Neighbors Thought).* New York: Harcourt, Brace & Company, 1997.

The Lincoln Library of Sports Champions. Volume 14. Columbus, OH: Frontier Press Company, 1993.

Owens, Jesse with Paul G. Neimark. *The Jesse Owens Story.* New York: G. P. Putnam's Sons, 1970.

Rennert, Rick. *Jesse Owens: Champion Athlete*. New York: Chelsea Juniors, 1992.

Sabin, Francene. *Jesse Owens: Olympic Hero.* New York: Troll Associates, 1986.

Sullivan, George. *Great Lives: Sports.* New York: Charles Scribner's Sons, 1988.

Leroy "Satchel" Paige

1906?-1982 • Baseball

Leroy Robert Page was born in Mobile, Alabama, the seventh of eleven children. His mother and father decided to change their last name from Page to Paige by adding an *i* because it would be more stylish.

When Leroy was seven, he got a job at the railroad station carrying baggage for the passengers. Since he was paid a dime for each piece he carried, he took a stick and rope and tied the luggage and satchels on it so he could carry more across his back. His friends began to call him "satchel tree." The name Satchel stuck with him. Later he got a job cleaning around the grandstand at the ballpark. Playing baseball soon became all he wanted to do. He couldn't afford a baseball, so he threw rocks and found he was very accurate. His mother asked him to kill a chicken for dinner, so he threw a rock and killed it with a blow to its head.

School was not his favorite place. He played hooky a lot and ran around with the wrong crowd. When he was 12, he saw toy rings in a store window, so he snatched them up and ran. But the owner caught him and called the police. In a day or so he was sent to the Industrial School for Negro Children and stayed there until he was 17.

He later commented that this turned out to be the best place for him. He had to go to school, he ate well, and he could now play baseball. He grew to 6 feet 3 inches tall and weighed 140 pounds. He was tall and thin, which earned him another nickname, "The Crane." When he left reform school in 1923, he began playing for an African American baseball team, the Mobile Tigers.

Satchel had a terrific fast ball and could put the ball wherever he wanted. Sometimes he would line up 10 soda bottles at home plate and knock down each one in order. He also practiced by throwing a baseball through a hole—the size of a man's hat—in a wooden fence. For years he traveled around the country playing in the Negro Leagues. The teams for which he played won the Negro League championships year after year. In the off-season he went south to the Dominican Republic, Mexico, Puerto Rico, and Venezuela to play. He made good money but did not spend it wisely and saved none of it. He bought cars, shotguns, and dogs. In 1947 he married Lahoma Brown, and they had five children over the next 12 years.

What he wanted most was to play in the major leagues. It wasn't until Jackie Robinson broke the color barrier that he was to receive his chance. In July 1948, Satchel signed with the Cleveland Indians. He was the oldest "rookie" at about 42 years of age. That year he won six games and only lost one. Cleveland won the American League Championship and the 1948 World Series, making him the first African American pitcher in a World Series. Later, Satchel would be the first African American inducted into the Baseball Hall of Fame.

Reading

1. Read a biography of Jackie Robinson. Compare and contrast Jackie and Satchel.
2. Read another biography of Satchel Paige from the Further Reading List. Discuss three things about him that were not brought out or explained fully in this biography.
3. Satchel Paige often spoke with humor. One of his lines was "Don't look back. Something may be gaining on you." What does that mean to you? Share your interpretation of that remark with your friends.

Social Studies

1. During the off-season in baseball (winter in the United States), Satchel played in the Dominican Republic, Mexico, Puerto Rico, and Venezuela. Find these countries on a map or globe. Which one is a commonwealth of the United States?
2. What are the two professional major leagues in the United States?
3. Pretend Satchel Paige arrived in one of his automobiles to spend the afternoon with you. Where would you suggest you go together in your community? Discuss your answer with your classmates.
4. You have just entered your school classroom or the living room of your home. Satchel looks up and smiles at you and asks if you have any questions you would like to ask him. List the first three questions that come to your mind. Discuss them with your friends or parents.

Further Reading

Brashler, William. *The Story of Negro League Baseball.* New York: Ticknor & Fields, 1994.

Cooper, Michael L. *Playing America's Game: The Story of Negro League Baseball.* New York: Lodestar Books, 1993.

Dunnahoo, Terry Janson and Herma Silverstein. *Baseball Hall of Fame.* New York: Crestwood House, 1994.

Geng, Don. *Fundamental Baseball.* Minneapolis, MN: Lerner Publications, 1995.

Kalb, Jonah. *How to Play Baseball Better Than You Did Last Season.* New York: Macmillan Publishing Co., 1974.

The Lincoln Library of Sports Champions. Volume 14. Columbus, OH: Frontier Press Company, 1993.

Macht, Norman L. *Satchel Paige.* New York: Chelsea House Publishers, 1991.

McKissack, Patricia and Fredrick. *Satchel Paige: The Best Arm in Baseball.* Hillside, NJ: Enslow Publishers, 1992.

Osborn, Kevin. *Scholastic Encyclopedia of Sports in the United States.* New York: Scholastic, 1997.

Shirley, David. *Satchel Paige: Baseball Great.* New York: Chelsea House Publishers, 1993.

The little boy born in a village in Brazil had more than one name. His parents called him Edson Arantes do Nascinmento and nicknamed him Dico. When he was eight, his playmates called him Pelé. No one knows where that name came from, but it stayed with him.

When he was a child, Pelé kicked a ball of rags, a sock filled with newspapers, or a grapefruit. He grew up wanting to be a soccer player like his father, Dindinho. Dindinho played professionally until an injury sidelined him. But he taught Pelé well.

Money was scarce in the family. Pelé quit school in the fourth grade to work part-time and help the family as well as to play soccer. He learned to pass the ball to the other players, use his head to punch the ball into the net, and even bounce the ball off the legs of his opponents!

Part of Pelé's ability was his peripheral vision as he raced down the field. He could see to his right and left, even though his eyes focused ahead. Pelé controlled the ball with his feet. He was also intelligent. Even though he dropped out of school, he later continued his education through high school and college, learned to speak five languages, played the guitar, and had a number of songs published.

Brazil selected Pelé to be on its World Cup team. The World Cup is an international competition held every four years. Brazil won the Cup in 1958, 1962, and 1970. The country wanted to make sure Pelé never played for another country's team before he retired, so in 1972 the government declared Pelé a "national treasure." By law he could not play for anyone else.

Outside the United States many countries call soccer "football." About ten times more people in the world watch soccer's World Cup than watch the Super Bowl. At one time, in the African country of Nigeria, there was a civil war going on between Nigeria and Biafra (a part of the country trying to establish its own government). Since Pelé was on a team coming to play there, the warring factions declared a truce for two or three days so the people on both sides could see him play. After the teams played, the war began anew.

When Pelé scored his thousandth goal, the people stood and cheered him for 11 minutes. In the course of his soccer career, he scored 1,281 goals in 1,363 games.

After he retired, Pelé accepted an invitation to come to the United States and play for the New York Cosmos for three years. By playing for the Cosmos, he encouraged U.S. citizens, especially children, to pursue the game. By doing so, he gave soccer a big boost.

Pelé was careful to be a role model for young people. He wrote in his autobiography: "I never endorsed a product I did not believe in or use, and I never endorsed any product that had any connection with tobacco or liquor of any type."

Reading

1. In order of importance, make a list of three character traits you think Pelé possesses. Compare your list with those of your classmates.
2. Write a sentence using 13 different words and tell something you learned about Pelé. Exchange your sentence with friends.
3. In your opinion, what other male athlete is or was most like Pelé? In what way?
4. What one thing impressed you most about Pelé? Compare your answer with the answers of your classmates.

Social Studies

1. What is the official language of Brazil?
2. Read about the World Cup in a reference book. Which country has won the World Cup the most number of times? Has the United States ever won? Jot down two other interesting facts you find out from your reading.
3. How do you feel about well-known personalities advertising products they do not use? Would you? Under what circumstances?
4. Read about Brazil in a reference book. If you were to visit there, what place would you prefer to go to first? Why?

Further Reading

Arnold, Caroline. *Pelé: The King of Soccer.* New York: Franklin Watts, 1992.

_____. *Soccer: From Neighborhood Play to the World Cup.* New York: Franklin Watts, 1991.

Brodman, Jonathon, editor. *Athletes.* Volume 2. Danbury, CT: Grolier, 1996.

Coleman, Lori. *Fundamental Soccer.* Minneapolis, MN: Lerner Publications, 1995.

Gutman, Bill. *Pelé.* New York: Grosset & Dunlap, 1976.

Krull, Kathleen. *Lives of the Athletes: Thrills, Spills (and What the Neighbors Thought).* New York: Harcourt, Brace & Company, 1997.

The Lincoln Library of Sports Champions. Volume 14. Columbus, OH: Frontier Press Company, 1993.

Marshall, David. *Soccer.* Crystal Lake, IL: Rigby Interactive Library, 1997.

Sullivan, George. *Great Lives: Sports.* New York: Charles Scribner's Sons, 1988.

Wilner, Barry. Soccer: *How to Play the All-Star Way.* Austin, TX: Raintree Steck-Vaughn, 1994.

Richard Petty

1937 • Automobile Racing

In the summer of 1942, in Level Cross, North Carolina, five-year-old Richard Petty could not believe his ears. His Uncle Bob asked him to drive the old Ford truck through the hay field while the men tossed the hay bales on it. He couldn't wait to get behind the wheel!

The Pettys were poor, as were most of the people in the area south of Greensboro. No one thought too much about their lack of electricity, running water, or telephone. They worked hard, went to church on Sunday, and ate well at the house of one set of grandparents in the afternoon and at the house of the other on Sunday evening.

Richard's father, Lee Petty, drove a delivery truck for a living. When he was 35, he began to race cars. About that time an organization called NASCAR (the National Association of Stock Car Auto Racing) was created. Lee quit the delivery business and started a machine shop. When Richard and his brother, Maurice, were older, they worked for their dad as mechanics and became his pit crew on weekends.

Richard knew what he wanted to do: race cars. But his dad sternly said he must wait until he was 21. Richard remained quiet about racing and pursued three sports in high school: football, basketball, and baseball. He did well in each. When he graduated from high school, he worked full-time for Petty Enterprises, the name of his father's business.

At 21, he asked his father again if he could race. Lee gave him a used 1957 Oldsmobile to fix up and take to the track. The number of his father's car was 42. Richard chose number 43 for his car. In Richard's first race, he came in sixth.

In 1959 Richard married a girl from his high school. They had a son and three daughters. Soon Richard was winning more races, even beating his father at times. In 1961 Lee injured his leg in a crash and later retired. Richard's pit crew, who kept his car running during a race, consisted of his brother, Maurice, his father, and other relatives.

By the end of the 1960s, stock-car racing had increased in popularity. Cars raced 170 miles per hour on the NASCAR tracks. Safety became important, for more and more drivers were becoming seriously injured at these high speeds. The improvements in race cars were put into passenger cars as well.

When Richard was 30, he had his best year. He won 27 races and came in second in seven others. Seventy-seven percent of the time he won or placed second! Sportswriters called him "The King."

Richard suffered many injuries; broken bones, broken ribs, a broken neck, a fractured shoulder, and the loss of some of his hearing. In 1991, at age 54, he retired after a 35-year career. He had won 200 races. He won the Daytona 500 seven times, and his earnings totaled $7,757,064. In 1992 he received the Medal of Freedom, the highest award given a U.S. civilian.

Reading

1. Of the five major kinds of automobile races (Formula One, sports car, Indy car, stock car, and drag), which one is most interesting to you? Explain to your classmates why you chose the one you did.
2. Write a dialogue with a race car you are driving at the Daytona 500 or Indianapolis 500. What would you say to each other as you see the checkered flag being raised and you come down the track together?
3. Make a list of the pluses and minuses of automobile car racing.
4. Draw a picture of the race car of the future. Give the race car a name.

Social Studies

1. Two famous races in the United States are the Indianapolis 500 and the Daytona 500. Read about them in a reference book and relate to your classmates two or three facts that you found interesting.
2. Locate the places on a map or globe where the above races are held. Which one is closest and farthest from your home?
3. Compare and contrast the sport of automobile racing with that of thoroughbred horse racing.
4. If you have access to the Internet, read about Richard Petty and tell your parents or friends what you learned.

Further Reading

Burchard, Marshall and Sue. *Sports Hero: Richard Petty.* New York: G. P. Putnam's Sons, 1974.

De Vere, Charles. *Let's Look Up Racing Cars.* New York: Gloucester Press, 1992.

Dolan, Edward F. Jr. *Great Moments in the Indy 500.* New York: Franklin Watts, 1982.

Frankel, Ron. *Richard Petty.* New York: Chelsea House Publishers, 1996.

Krishef, Robert K. *The Indianapolis 500.* Minneapolis, MN: Lerner Publications, 1974.

The Lincoln Library of Sports Champions. Volume 14. Columbus, OH: Frontier Press Company, 1993.

Murphy, Jim. *The Indy 500.* New York: Clarion Books, 1983.

Olney, Ross R. *Super Champions of Auto Racing.* New York: Clarion Books, 1984.

Fairmont, West Virginia, a coal mining industrial town, is 90 miles south of Pittsburgh, Pennsylvania, along the Monongahela River. Mary Lou Retton was born there. Her father, Ronnie, played shortstop for a New York Yankees farm team for a few years. Her mother, Lois, noticed that Mary Lou not only walked at nine months of age, but she did it without stumbling or falling.

With three older brothers and a sister, all with athletic ability, Mary Lou was constantly involved in physical exercise. The running and tumbling around the house finally led Lois to send Mary Lou and her sister to dancing school for ballet, tap dancing, and acrobatics. Stocky and short by her own admission, Mary Lou turned to gymnastics when she was five. At age 13, she won the all-around international gymnastics competition.

Mary Lou realized she needed more intensive training if she were to become an Olympic medal winner. Finally, after months of pleading and discussion, her parents allowed her to train with Bela Karolyi. He and his wife had defected from Romania to the United States and opened a gymnastic training center in Houston, Texas. Bela had trained Nadia Comeneci, a gold-medal winner in the 1976 Olympics. Not yet 15, Mary Lou began training for the 1984 Olympic Games.

Seven days a week, training in the morning and evening, Mary Lou learned new techniques and unlearned bad ones she had developed. Her social life was put on hold, for she had no time for dating. There were other sacrifices, too, such as her schooling. She dropped out of school and took a correspondence course to finish high school. She missed her family, but her mother wrote her every day. Mary Lou gained confidence and skill during these months of intense Olympic preparation.

Then, just six weeks before the Olympics, Mary Lou injured her right leg. Cartilage fragments caught in the knee and she was unable to bend it. Arthroscopic surgery was performed. The doctors thought she could not heal in time for the Olympic games, but within a few days she was back practicing harder than ever.

The 23rd Olympic Games were held in Los Angeles in the summer of 1984. Whether Mary Lou would win a gold medal depended on her last event, the vault. She had two chances. The best score of the two would determine her success. On her first try, she got a perfect 10. She did it again, just to show she could, and got the same score. Mary Lou won her gold medal by just .05 of a point against a Romanian competitor! Altogether, she won five medals in gymnastics: one gold, two silver, and two bronze.

The people in Fairmont were ecstatic. Someone even stole the Retton mailbox for a souvenir. Others dug plots of grass from the yard. Mary Lou received so much fan mail that it was put in large plastic bags, waiting for her to find time to answer. To top it off, her picture on a Wheaties™ cereal box was a first for a female athlete.

Reading

1. Are there any incidents in the life of Mary Lou Retton that remind you of something that has happened in your life? If so, what? Share with your classmates.

2. What is the most important word, phrase, or sentence in the biography of Mary Lou Retton? Explain to your classmates why you chose it.

3. Read biographies of Olga Korbut and Nadia Comeneci. Compare and contrast their lives with Mary Lou's. How do you think they are alike and different?

4. Famous people, especially athletes, have little privacy when they are in public settings. How do you think you would act if you were seated close to a celebrity in a restaurant? Discuss your views with friends.

Social Studies

1. On a physical map trace the Monongahela River from Fairmont, West Virginia, through Pittsburgh, Pennsylvania, and to the sea. Into what two rivers and large body of water does it flow?

2. Read about West Virginia in a reference book. Make a list of the five most interesting things you learned. Compare them with those things your classmates found.

3. Read about arthroscopy in a reference book. Explain how doctors use it to help their patients who have shoulder, elbow, hip, and knee joint problems.

4. In an almanac, or some other reference, find the location of the next Summer and Winter Olympic Games. Learn several things of interest about each place and share the information with your classmates.

Further Reading

Berke, Art. *Gymnastics.* New York: Franklin Watts, 1988.

Cohen, Joel H. *Super Stars of Women's Gymnastics.* Philadelphia, PA: Chelsea House Publishers, 1997.

Kent, Zachary. *U.S. Olympians.* Chicago, IL: Childrens Press, 1992.

The Lincoln Library of Sports Champions. Volume 15. Columbus, OH: Frontier Press Company, 1993.

Retton, Mary Lou and Bela Karolyi with John Powers. *Mary Lou: Creating an Olympic Champion.* New York: McGraw-Hill Book Company, 1986.

Silverstein, Herma. *Mary Lou Retton and the New Gymnasts*. New York: Franklin Watts, 1985.

Sullivan, George. *Mary Lou Retton.* New York: Julian Messner, 1984.

Washington, Rosemary G. *Mary Lou Retton: Power Gymnast.* Minneapolis, MN: Lerner Publications, 1985.

Woolum, Janet. *Outstanding Women Athletes: Who They Are and How They Influenced Sports in America.* Phoenix, AZ: The Oryx Press, 1992.

Jack "Jackie" Robinson | 1919-1972 • BASEBALL

Jackie was 16 months old when his mother took him, three brothers, and one sister on the long train ride from Cairo, Georgia, to Pasadena, California. They went there to live in a three-room apartment with an uncle's family. Jackie's father had deserted them. Jackie's mother, Mallie, did laundry to earn money and saved enough to purchase a home for her children. Often they ate day-old bread soaked in sugar water.

Because Jackie's mother worked long hours to support her family, Jackie went to school with his sister when he was 4 years old. He played in the sandbox outside the school until she was finished for the day. Then they went home together.

All of the Robinson children did well in athletic activities. Jackie's brother, Mack, won an Olympic silver medal in Berlin, Germany, when he came in second in the 200-meter dash. The winner was another African American, Jesse Owens.

Jackie went to Pasadena Junior College for two years. On one particular day he set a record in the broad jump (25 feet 6 inches) and then was driven 40 miles to help the baseball team win a championship!

The next two years he went to UCLA and became the first athlete in the school's history to win letters in four sports: football, basketball, baseball, and track. Jackie was drafted into the army in World War II and became an officer. When discharged in 1945, he decided to play professional baseball. African Americans were not permitted to play on the white professional teams, so they organized their own leagues. Jackie joined the Kansas City Monarchs of the Negro Baseball League.

Branch Rickey was made president of the Brooklyn Dodgers in 1943. He planned to break the color barrier, an invisible wall that kept African Americans and other players of color out of the major leagues. He learned about Jackie Robinson and called him to his office in New York City. They talked for nearly three hours. At the end, Jackie promised not to show anger and fight back when he was verbally abused by the fans and other teams on or off the field. Mr. Rickey told him, "I want a man with guts enough not to fight back."

He spent the first year playing with the Dodgers' farm team, the Montreal Royals in Canada. Jackie and the Royals won their championship. He moved up to the Brooklyn Dodgers in 1947 and became the first African American to play in modern major league baseball.

Jackie did so well with the Dodgers that he was named the National League Rookie of the Year. His running and base stealing made him a favorite of many fans. By 1949, he won the National League's Most Valuable Player award and the league's batting championship with a .342 average. On July 23, 1962, he was elected to the National Baseball Hall of Fame in Cooperstown, New York. Ten years later, at the age of 53, he died of diabetes and heart problems.

Reading

1. Which paragraph is the most important one in the biography? Defend your choice before your classmates.
2. Discuss Branch Rickey's statement: "I want a man with guts enough not to fight back." Why did he make that statement and what did he mean by it?
3. Write three titles for this biography. Arrange them in order of importance.
4. With a classmate, write a "conversation-about Jackie." First, each of you write a statement about him. Next, exchange statements and write your replies. Do this three or four times. Then discuss what both of you wrote.

Social Studies

1. On a map, place a ruler to show a straight line from Cairo, Georgia, to Pasadena, California. List the states Mallie Robinson and her children may have traveled through by train to get to the West Coast.
2. As the first African American to break baseball's color barrier, Jackie had to endure taunting from his opponents, heckling from fans and even hate mail and death threats. How do you think he managed to keep his cool and focus on baseball? How would you have responded under that kind of pressure?
3. Draw several pictures of Jackie Robinson at different places and times as a young person and baseball player. Label each picture with a caption telling where the scene is located and what it is about. Tell what is happening as you show the pictures to your classmates.
4. Create a book jacket for Jackie Robinson's biography. Use the information in this and other biographies to create a cover that captures Jackie's life and career.

Further Reading

Bennett, William J. *The Children's Book of Heroes*. New York: Simon & Schuster, 1997.

Brashler, William. *The Story of Negro League Baseball.* New York: Ticknor & Fields, 1994.

Coombs, Karen Mueller. *Jackie Robinson: Baseball's Civil Rights Legend.* Springfield, NJ: Enslow Publishers, 1997.

Grabowski, John. *Jackie Robinson.* New York: Chelsea House Publishers, 1991.

Greene, Carol. *Jackie Robinson: Baseball's First Black Major-Leaguer.* Chicago, IL: Childrens Press, 1990.

Krull, Kathleen. *Lives of the Athletes: Thrills, Spills (and What the Neighbors Thought).* New York: Harcourt, Brace & Company, 1997.

The Lincoln Library of Sports Champions. Volume 15. Columbus, OH: Frontier Press Company, 1993.

Reiser, Howard. *Jackie Robinson: Baseball Pioneer.* New York: Franklin Watts, 1992.

Sanford, William R. and Carl R. Greene. *Jackie Robinson.* New York: Crestwood House, 1992.

Santella, Andrew. *Jackie Robinson Breaks the Color Line.* New York: Childrens Press, 1996.

Sullivan, George. *Great Lives: Sports.* New York: Charles Scribner's Sons, 1988.

Wilma Rudolph

1940-1994 • TRACK AND FIELD

Wilma was born weighing 4½ pounds. When she was four years old, she contracted double pneumonia and scarlet fever. If that was not enough, polio affected one of her legs to the point where she needed a brace to walk.

Her mother, Blanche, took her by bus to a medical college some 50 miles away twice a week. There therapists worked to help strengthen her leg. At home, her mother and her many brothers and sisters massaged the leg. Then one Sunday morning, unknown to her family, she took off her brace. Ten-year-old Wilma then walked down the center aisle of the church to sit with her family! By the next year the brace was packed and sent back to the hospital.

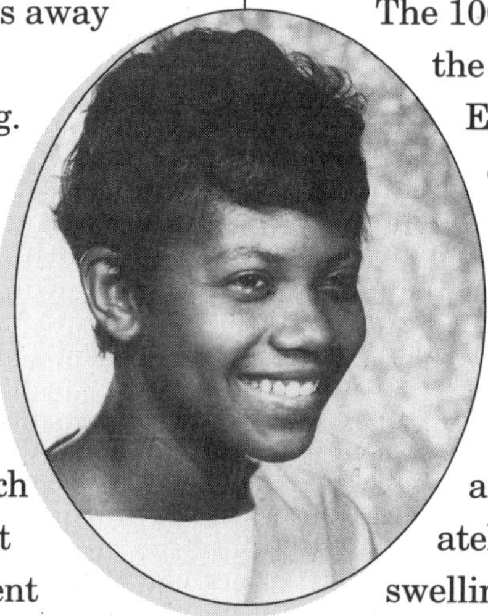

Ed Temple, the track coach at Tennessee State University, refereed high school basketball in Tennessee. He was always on the lookout for budding track stars and saw such potential in Wilma. He encouraged her family to allow Wilma to attend his summer program for high school runners in 1956. She was so fast that she was invited to try out for the Olympics. In Melbourne, she earned a bronze medal as a member of the 400-meter relay team.

Wilma came back to her high school. By now she was a 6-foot, barely 90-pound heroine. She was so quick on the basketball court that her coach nicknamed her "Skeeter" because she resembled a mosquito buzzing around. Averaging around 32 points a game, she looked forward to the 1960 Olympics.

Even so, going to college as an athlete was not always easy. Illness, a pulled muscle, and a tonsillectomy affected her performance. Wilma persevered. She set a world record in the 200-meter dash of 22.9 seconds as she prepared for the Rome Olympics. At 20 years of age, she went to the 1960 Olympics in Italy. The 100-degree heat was oppressive to the athletes. Fortunately, her coach, Ed Temple, was named as the coach of the track and field team. He decided the women should do light workouts. As Wilma and the others ran in the grass among the cooling lawn sprinklers, Wilma stepped into a hole and sprained her ankle. Immediately ice was applied to stop the swelling. The next day her foot held up and she qualified for the 100-meter dash. The following day she won a gold medal in the race. Then she won the 200-meter race with a time of 23.3 seconds, an Olympic record. Later, as anchor in the 400-meter race, Wilma came from behind to set another record and win three gold medals. She was the first woman athlete ever to accomplish this.

Wilma Rudolph was known as the fastest woman in the world. She returned to college, graduated, became an elementary school teacher, married, and later wrote her autobiography, which became a TV movie. She established the Wilma Rudolph Foundation, an organization that helps young people to become dedicated athletes and citizens.

Reading

1. Act out the scene where Wilma walks down the church aisle without her brace. Ask your friends to take the parts of Wilma, her mother, her father, and the preacher. What do they say and do?
2. Who is the fastest runner in your class? Ask your teacher to set up races to find out.
3. How are you most like and unlike Wilma Rudolph? How do your times in the 100-meter and 200-meter races compare to Wilma's?
4. Write a diary page telling what Wilma might have written after practicing four years for the 1960 Olympics, only to sprain her ankle hours before the races. How would she feel? What would she write?

Social Studies

1. On a map or globe find the locations of the Melbourne, Australia and Rome, Italy, Olympics. Read about these cities in a reference book. Find things of interest about these two places and discuss what you found with your classmates.
2. What is the medical name for polio? What is now given to children to prevent this disease?
3. Talk to some older adults about the fastest runners they remember. Take notes. Discuss them with your classmates.
4. What was the most serious disease you had as a small child? How does it compare to those Wilma had?

Further Reading

Biracree, Tom. *Wilma Rudolph.* New York: Chelsea House Publishers, 1988.

Coffey, Wayne. *Wilma Rudolph*. Woodridge, CT: Blackbirch Press, 1993.

Jones, Betty Millsaps. *Wonder Women of Sports.* New York: Random House, 1981.

Kent, Zachary. *U.S. Olympians.* Chicago, IL: Childrens Press, 1992.

Krull, Kathleen. *Lives of the Athletes: Thrills, Spills (and What the Neighbors Thought).* New York: Harcourt, Brace & Company, 1997.

__________. *Wilma Unlimited: How Wilma Rudolph Became the World's Fastest Woman.* San Diego, CA: Harcourt Brace & Company, 1996.

The Lincoln Library of Sports Champions. Volume 15. Columbus, OH: Frontier Press Company, 1993.

O'Connor, Jim. *Comeback: Four True Stories.* New York: Random House, 1992.

Rudolph, Wilma with Martin Ralbovsky. *Wilma*. New York: New American Library, 1977.

Sherrow, Victoria. *Wilma Rudolph: Olympic Champion.* New York: Chelsea Juniors, 1995.

Wickham, Martha. *Superstars of Women's Track and Field.* New York: Chelsea House Publishers, 1997.

Woolum, Janet. *Outstanding Women Athletes: Who They Are and How They Influenced Sports in America.* Phoenix, AZ: The Oryx Press, 1992.

Bernice Sayers wanted her second child to be a girl. She chose Gail as a name for the new baby. When she and her husband, Roger, had a boy, they named him "Gale," with a masculine spelling.

By the time Gale was eight, the family had moved from Wichita, Kansas, to Omaha, Nebraska. There was never enough money to pay the bills, so Gale helped out by delivering newspapers. Because chicken feet were inexpensive, the family ate them often, fried and stewed. Gale's BB gun accounted for sparrows and catbirds, which became part of the family's diet.

Gale slept in the hallway near the kitchen because of lack of room. They used the kitchen stove as a source of heat. Just outside was an alley nearly the length of a football field. It was there Gale spent much of his time, even into the dark, playing football. It became his passion.

His first year at Omaha Central High School, practice began at 6:30 in the morning. Gale loved it. Track in the spring rounded out his year as an athlete. High school classes were not nearly as exciting and his grades reflected his disinterest. English was especially troublesome.

Gale was offered football scholarships to college. He decided to play for the University of Kansas. When he went home on weekends to visit his family, and especially his girlfriend, Linda, he cried knowing he had to return to campus. In 1962 he and Linda married, and she helped him to settle down and study. Hard work in his studies and on the football field, plus a regimen of year-round exercise training, turned him into an All-American on the football field in 1963 and 1964. More importantly, his grades bounced up to a B average in his senior year of college.

George Halas, the owner and coach of the Chicago Bears, persuaded Gale to play for Chicago. In his rookie season, he led the league in points scored (132), number of touchdowns (22), and total offensive yards (2,275). Not only that, Gale was an excellent kick returner, pass receiver and running back. But it was on December 12, 1965, that he tied the National Football League record when he scored six touchdowns in one game! He was named Rookie of the Year.

Gale's roommate on the Bears was Brian Piccolo. Brian became ill with lung cancer. When the Pro Football writers gave Gale their award for "the most courageous player," Gale announced he was giving the award the next day to his good friend, Brian. Soon after, Brian died. The memory of their close friendship was kept alive by the made-for-TV film *Brian's Song*.

Four operations on his knees compelled Gale to stop competing on the football field. He then studied for and passed a stockbroker's exam. Gale went on to work at various colleges and helped students solve their problems. In 1977 Gale Sayers was inducted into the Pro Football Hall of Fame in Canton, Ohio.

Reading

1. In other references or books, read the list of records Gale set. To you, which one is most important? Why?
2. What kind of person does Gale Sayers appear to be? Would you like him for a friend? Why or why not?
3. Gale Sayers tied the number of touchdowns (6) scored in a single game in pro football. In a reference book, find out what Red Grange did in a 1925 college game, as a running back, when the University of Illinois played against Michigan. Share what you find with your classmates.

Social Studies

1. Read about the history of U.S. football in a reference book. Prepare five facts to share with your classmates.
2. Wichita, Kansas; Omaha, Nebraska; and Chicago, Illinois, are three places Gale Sayers called home. Prepare three interesting facts about each place and report to your classmates what you learned. Find each place on a U.S. map. Which of the cities is nearest you?
3. Which high school, college, and/or professional football players are your favorites? Share your selections with your classmates. Do they agree with you?

Further Reading

Cox, Ted. *Football.* Crystal Lake, IL: Rigby Interactive Library, 1996.

Hahn, James and Lynn. *Sayers! The Sports Career of Gale Sayers.* Mankato, MN: Crestwood House, 1981.

Italia, Bob. *The Chicago Bears*. Edina, MN: Abdo & Daughters, 1996.

_______. 100 *Unforgettable Moments in Pro Football. 100 Unforgettable Moments in Sports.* Edina, MN: Abdo & Daughters, 1996.

The Lincoln Library of Sports Champions. Volume 12. Columbus, OH: Frontier Press Company, 1993.

Madden, John. *The First Book of Football.* New York: Crown Publishers, 1988.

May, Julian. *Gale Sayers: Star Running Back.* Mankato, MN: Crestwood House, 1975.

Raffo, Dave. *Football: How to Play the All-Star Way.* Austin, TX: Raintree Steck-Vaughn, Publishers, 1994.

Sullivan, George. *All About Football.* New York: Dodd, Mead & Company, 1987.

Arnold was born in a little country village outside of Graz, Austria. He was frail during much of his childhood. His father, Gustav, encouraged him and his older brother, Meinhart, to do squats and situps for 15 minutes before breakfast each morning.

As a hobby, the father lifted weights and invited his sons to do the same. He also stimulated the mental processes of his sons by making them write ten-page essays after their Sunday afternoon excursions to a museum or park. The next morning, he would correct the papers. If there were errors, the boys would have to correct and, often, rewrite them.

By the age of 15, Arnold became quite interested in bodybuilding. He worked out daily at the Athletic Union. One Monday morning, the caretaker of the building found a window smashed on the second floor. Arnold confessed to breaking into the building on the weekend so he could train seven days a week!

Arnold enjoyed other sports, too, besides lifting weights. He played soccer, skied, boxed, and did curling. At 15 he weighed 160 pounds. At 18 he was in the Austrian army driving a tank. In the army he continued his weight training and was able to eat more food, especially meat. At one point he went absent without leave to enter the Junior Mr. Europe contest in Germany. He won but had to spend several days as a prisoner on his return to duty.

His bodybuilding friends nicknamed him "the Austrian Oak." At 18 he won the Austrian Junior Olympics championship. In the 1960s, he won the Mr. Universe contest five years in a row. But all this did not satisfy Arnold's desire for success. As part of his master plan, he focused on becoming the best body builder ever, learning perfect English, investing in real estate, becoming a movie star, and making a fortune.

At the height of his body-building career, Arnold weighed 240 pounds, was 6 feet 2 inches tall, had a chest measurement of 57 inches, a 31-inch waist, 22-inch biceps, 28-inch thighs, and 20-inch calves. He came to the United States and turned professional and won many titles.

His goal of becoming a movie star was reached when he appeared in action movies such as *Conan the Barbarian, The Terminator*, and *Commando*. He also did comedies such as *Kindergarten Cop* and *Twins,* the latter making more than $100 million in less than a month. That helped him considerably with his goal of making a fortune!

Arnold married Maria Shriver, a television broadcaster, and became a father. Maria's mother, Eunice, was the sister of John, Robert, and Teddy Kennedy. Arnold and Maria named their first baby Katherine Eunice.

In 1990 Arnold was made chairman of the President's Council of Physical Fitness and Sports, touring America and talking to boys and girls about keeping physically fit.

Reading

1. Arnold was quite good at the sport of curling as a youngster. Read about curling in a dictionary or reference book and tell your classmates or friends what you learned about the sport. Is it played in your state?
2. Read about Maria's uncles, John, Robert, and Ted Kennedy, in a reference book. What positions of influence did they have?
3. With a cloth tape measure, compare and contrast your body measurements with those of Arnold's.
4. Arnold's body building friends nicknamed him "the Austrian oak." Why do you think they chose that term? What would you like to be called as an athlete?

Social Studies

1. Find Graz, Austria, on a map or globe: latitude 47° 5 N; longitude 15° 22 E.
2. What is the greatest need, in terms of fitness, for the boys and girls in your community? Discuss this need in your class.
3. Arnold had a "master plan" worked out for his life. Make a list of the goals you would like to achieve in the future. Keep it some place where you can review it from time to time. What can you do this week to work toward accomplishing your goals?

Further Reading

Conklin, Thomas. *Meet Arnold Schwarzenegger.* New York: Random House, 1994.

The Lincoln Library of Sports Champions. Volume 16. Columbus, OH: Frontier Press Company, 1993.

Lipsyte, Robert. *Arnold Schwarzenegger: Hercules in America.* New York: HarperCollinsPublishers, 1993.

Lund, Bill. *Weight Lifting.* Mankato, MN: Capstone Press, 1996.

Meeks, Christopher. *Arnold Schwarzenegger: Hard Work Brought Success.* Vero Beach, FL: The Rourke Corporation, 1993.

North, Jack. *Arnold Schwarzenegger.* New York: Dillon Press, 1994.

Schwarzenegger, Arnold with Charles Gaines. *Arnold's Fitness for Kids ages 6–10: A Guide to Health, Exercise, and Nutrition.* New York: Doubleday, 1993.

Schwarzenegger, Arnold with Charles Gaines. *Arnold's Fitness for Kids ages 11–14: A Guide to Health, Exercise, and Nutrition.* New York: Doubleday, 1993.

Bill was born small. The doctor who delivered him didn't expect the 2½-pound baby to make it through the night. But his grandma warmed the oven, tucked him into some pillows on the stove door, and sat with him throughout the night. His aunt thought he looked like a rat with his long black hair.

When he was four or five, he was left alone for a few moments. It was enough time for him to climb a fence and jump on a nearby horse. Bill gave it a kick and walked the horse around the corral. His mother and a few relatives panicked.

Bill enjoyed boxing and wrestling in school. A girl suggested that, because he was so small, he should consider becoming a jockey. Since he liked horses, he got a job feeding and exercising the horses and cleaning stalls. He also washed, combed, and brushed the animals. This was the life he wanted to pursue, so he dropped out of school to become a jockey.

Jockeys need to be small to race thoroughbred horses. Bill was built for the job. For most of his life he weighed 97 pounds. On the day of a race the stewards added lead weights on his saddle so his weight compared to the other jockeys who were racing. Once when he vacationed in Acapulco, Mexico, he did increase his weight to 103 pounds!

As Bill began to win races, sportswriters gave him various nicknames: "Wee Willie," "Willie the Shoe," and "Silent Shoe." Bill's front teeth were a bit crooked, so he often kept silent during interviews. Later a dentist capped his teeth for $10,000 and he began smiling a lot. He thought capping was a good investment.

One time when he rode in the Kentucky Derby, Bill made a big mistake. He thought he had crossed the finish line, so he started to stand up in the stirrups of his horse. But there was still a little distance to go. His horse lost by just a few inches. Bill made a public apology for his mistake. Nevertheless, he was suspended from racing for 15 days.

There were two times Bill was seriously hurt as a jockey. Once he fell with his horse in a race. The horse hit him in the right thigh, breaking the long bone, the femur. In the children's department at the hospital, the doctors found a metal rod that fit the hollow parts of the break and held it together. After his dismissal from the hospital, he lifted weights, rode a stationary bicycle, and ran. He was out of racing for more than a year, but the first day back he won three races.

Another time, he was trapped under a horse before a race. His pelvis bone splintered in five places. He also had a ruptured bladder and a paralyzed leg. But he came back again.

When Bill retired in 1990, he had ridden 8,883 winners in more than 40,000 races. He rode Kentucky Derby winning horses in four different years, his last win when he was 54 years old, the oldest jockey to win the Derby. Unfortunately, in 1991 a car accident left him paralyzed and in a wheelchair. Undaunted, Bill writes horse-racing mystery novels.

Reading

1. How did your understanding of the biography change your feeling about race horse jockeys? Share your thoughts with your classmates.
2. Write three questions you would like Bill Shoemaker to answer. Read them aloud to your classmates and let them tell you what answers Bill might give.
3. In a reference book, find the dates Bill won the Kentucky Derby. List the years and the names of the horses. In your mind, which horse had the most interesting name? Why?

Social Studies

1. Bill publicly admitted a mistake he made when riding in the Kentucky Derby. Have you ever made a mistake for which you took responsibility? How did you feel?
2. Find Acapulco, Mexico, on a map. What body of water does it border?
3. From a reference book, read about the many records Bill Shoemaker set as a jockey. Which two are most important in your mind? Discuss this with your classmates or parents.
4. Read about thoroughbred racing in a reference book or juvenile book. List five interesting facts you learned and share them with your classmates.

Further Reading

Forbis, Judith E. *Hoofbeats Along the Tigris.* Mena, AR: Ansata Publications, 1990.

Harris, Jack C. *The Kentucky Derby.* Mankato, MN: Creative Education, 1990.

Johnson, Neil. *Born to Run: A Racehorse Grows Up.* New York: Scholastic, 1988.

The Lincoln Library of Sports Champions. Volume 16. Columbus, OH: Frontier Press Company, 1993.

McFarland, Cynthia. *Hoofbeats: The Story of a Thoroughbred.* New York: Atheneum, 1993.

Phillips, Louis. *Willie Shoemaker.* Mankato, MN: Crestwood House, 1988.

Stone, Lynn M. *Bluegrass Country.* Vero Beach, FL: Rourke Corporation, 1993.

Amos Alonzo Stagg | 1862-1965 • Football

Amos Alonzo Stagg was the fifth child in a family of eight children. He never drank alcoholic beverages, smoked, nor swore. Each November, his father butchered two pigs. The pigs made, among other things, the sausage that went with the daily breakfast of buckwheat cakes. Amos asked his father for the pigs' bladders and blew them up for footballs.

In Amos's day, not many boys, nor girls, went to high school. Because he had to help at home, Amos didn't begin the eighth grade until he was 18 but finished his public schooling three years later. The assistant principal suggested college to Amos. Amos decided on Yale but could not pass the entrance exam. On the advice of a friend, Amos went to a preparatory academy. His friend gave him one of his suits, since Amos had none. Amos wanted no more help. When his Presbyterian minister bid him farewell, he held out his hand to shake Amos's hand. Amos saw money in the minister's hand, so he put out his other hand and wouldn't take the money. At the preparatory school he took the needed courses, pitched for the baseball team, and passed his Yale entrance exams.

At 22 years old with only $32, Amos entered Yale. He set a budget for himself: $1 a week for a drafty room and 20 cents a day for food. He became ill with malnutrition. A doctor ordered him to drop the "nickel- and-dime-meal nonsense." Amos got a job waiting tables in a student dining room where he could eat well.

Amos played on Yale's baseball team. He pitched for five championship games. In a game against the professional Boston Nationals, Amos beat them 2 to 1. In the ninth inning, he struck out their best hitter, Ten-Thousand-Dollar Kelly, the Babe Ruth of 1887. Amos also played right end for the 1888 Yale football team. They outscored their opponents 698 points to 0!

After a year in Yale's divinity school, Amos left because he felt he could not express himself well enough to be a minister. He went to the newly created University of Chicago as coach and head of its physical culture department. There, at 31, he met a freshman student, Stella Roberston, and they married. In the press box, she charted plays for him. That first year, as coach, he even played with the team because they were short of players.

Amos coached at Chicago from 1892 through 1932. He invented the tackling dummy and introduced the T-formation, onside kick, and double-reverse. When the forward pass became legal in 1906, Amos created more than 60 plays for using it.

When he was 70, the University of Chicago asked him to retire and be an advisor. Instead, he coached at the University of the Pacific, in California, until he was 81. He joined his son, Amos Jr., in Pennsylvania as an offensive coordinator until he was 90. He then took an advisory position at Stockton Junior College. And at 98, after 71 years of coaching, it was "time to stop." He lived to be 102.

Reading

1. What are the five most interesting facts in the biography of Amos Alonzo Stagg? Compare your list with those of your classmates.
2. Read a biography of Bear Bryant, Vince Lombardi, or Knute Rockne from the Further Reading list. Compare and contrast it with what you learned from your reading of Amos Alonzo Stagg's biography.
3. What is your belief on mandatory retirement from a profession at a specific age? Should a person be forced to retire at a set age? Why? Discuss your opinions with your classmates.
4. Read the biography of Amos Alonzo Stagg to a senior citizen or older relative or friend. Take notes on his or her reactions and discuss them with your classmates.

Social Studies

1. Name the wars in which the United States was engaged in the year Amos Alonzo Stagg was born (1862) and the year he died (1965).
2. Read about malnutrition in a reference book. Discuss with your classmates its effects on the human body.
3. Create a television commercial featuring Amos Alonzo Stagg at 98 years of age. What products would he most likely promote? Which ones would he not promote?
4. How are you most like Amos Alonzo Stagg? In what ways are you different? List and discuss answers with your classmates.

Further Reading

Allen, James. *Football: Play Like a Pro.* Mahwah, NJ: Troll Associates, 1990.

Anderson, Dave. *The Story of Football.* New York: William Morrow and Company, 1997.

Lloyd, Bryant. *Football: Rules of the Game.* Vero Beach, FL: The Rourke Book Company, Inc., 1997.

Madden, John. *The First Book of Football.* New York: Crown Publishers, 1988.

Osborn, Kevin. *Scholastic Encyclopedia of Sports in the United States.* New York: Scholastic, 1997.

Riper, Guernsey V., Jr. *Knute Rockne: Young Athlete.* Childhood of New York: Macmillan Publishing Co., 1986.

Smith, E. S. *Bear Bryant: Football's Winning Coach.* New York: Walker and Company, 1984.

Sullivan, George. *All About Football.* New York: Dodd, Mead & Company, 1987.

Wukovits, John. *Vince Lombardi.* Philadelphia, PA: Chelsea House Publishers, 1997.

Jim Thorpe

1887-1953 • Football, Baseball, Track and Field

Jim and Charlie were twins born in a cabin in Oklahoma. Jim was husky and enjoyed adventure; Charlie was quiet and thoughtful. The two boys of the Sac and Fox Indian tribe were good for each other. Charlie helped Jim in school; Jim protected Charlie. But at eight, Charlie died of pneumonia, leaving Jim broken-hearted.

School was not Jim's favorite place, for it was 20 miles or so from the family and farm. One day Jim left school, running all the way home. His father promptly put him in a wagon and took him back. By the time his father returned home, Jim had left again and was waiting for him!

Jim finally realized that school was the best place for him, so in 1904 he entered Carlisle Institute in Pennsylvania, a school for Native American young people.

Football attracted Jim but he was too small for such a rough game. One day as he watched the older boys on the track team fail to clear the high jump bar in practice, he asked if he could try. They laughed, but said sure. Jim did it in his school clothes on his first try and broke the school record.

"Pop" Warner, the coach, heard of his feat and put him on the track squad. But Jim wanted to play football, too. Finally, the coach said he would use him for varsity tackling practice. Jim began to run from the far end of the field toward the varsity players, eluding them all. Moments later he was alone at the other end. Pop could not believe it and told him to do it again. And Jim did. Jim muttered, "Nobody is going to tackle Jim." He was promoted to the football team.

Jim Thorpe went on to break records in football and track at Carlisle. In the summer, he played baseball in the South. Jim entered the 1912 Olympic Games in Stockholm, Sweden. There he won the decathlon and pentathlon track and field events. When King Gustav presented Jim his medals, the King said, "Sir, you are the greatest athlete in the world." Jim humbly said, "Thanks, King."

A few months later the newspapers reported that Jim had accepted small amounts of money playing summer baseball. This made him a professional and, therefore, ineligible to compete at the previous Olympics. He had to return his awards.

Jim went on to play professional football for the Canton Bulldogs and baseball for the Cleveland Indians, New York Giants, and Chicago Cardinals.

In 1950 the nation's press named him for two awards: the greatest athlete and the greatest football player of the half-century. In 1963 Jim was inducted as a charter member of the Pro Football Hall of Fame in Canton, Ohio. Every year the National Football League honors its most valuable player with the Jim Thorpe Trophy. The International Olympic Committee restored his Olympic records in 1982 and returned his medals to his family.

Reading

1. What would you have said if you were Jim and had just been told by a king that you were the greatest athlete in the world?
2. Who do you think is the greatest athlete of the second half century? The greatest football player? Compare your choices with those of your friends.
3. The decathlon, heptathlon, and pentathlon are combined competitions lasting one or two days. To win, the athlete must have a total score better than that of his or her competitors. With a friend, read about these competitions from a reference book. In which competition or event would you perform best?
4. Because Jim had earned $15 a week playing baseball early in his career, his Olympic Gold medals were taken away. Pretend you are Jim Thorpe. Write a journal entry that describes your thoughts and feelings upon finding out that the Olympic Committee wants you to turn over your gold medals.

Social Studies

1. Find Stockholm, Sweden, site of the 1912 Olympic Games, on a map or globe.
2. To your class or friends, report about the Sac (also spelled Sauk and Sak) and Fox Indians. Who was their famous chief in the 1832 war?
3. Debate the issue: Athletes who have earned money competing in their sport should or should not be able to compete in the Olympics.

Further Reading

Anderson, Dave. *The Story of Football.* New York: William Morrow and Company, 1997.

__________. *The Story of the Olympics.* New York: William Morrow and Company, 1996.

Bernotas, Bob. *Jim Thorpe: Sac and Fox Athlete.* New York: Chelsea House Publishers, 1992.

Kent, Zachary. *U.S. Olympians.* Chicago, IL: Childrens Press, 1992.

Knight, Theodore. *The Olympic Games.* San Diego, CA: Lucent Books, 1991.

Krull, Kathleen. *Lives of the Athletes: Thrills, Spills (and What the Neighbors Thought).* New York: Harcourt Brace & Company, 1997.

The Lincoln Library of Sports Champions. Volume 18. Columbus, OH: Frontier Press Company, 1993.

Lipsyte, Robert. *Jim Thorpe: 20th-Century Jock.* New York: HarperCollinsPublishers, 1993.

Osborn, Kevin. *Scholastic Encyclopedia of Sports in the United States.* New York: Scholastic, 1997.

Richards, Gregory. *Jim Thorpe: World's Greatest Athlete.* Chicago, IL: Childrens Press, 1984.

Sullivan, George. *Great Lives: Sports.* New York: Charles Scribner's Sons, 1988.

Updyke, Rosemary, K. *Jim Thorpe: The Legend Remembered.* Gretna, LA: Pelican Publishing Company, 1997.

Kristi was quite small at birth: 5 pounds 15 ounces. She was born with clubfeet, a condition where her toes turned inward. This affected her walking, so she had to wear corrective shoes, take physical therapy, and wear a special brace at night, which was painful.

The little California girl was four years old when she and her mother stopped to watch the ice skaters at a shopping mall ice rink. Kristi was entranced and begged her mother to allow her to skate. Yes, her mother promised, when you go to first grade.

Kristi's mother, who is of Japanese descent, was born in a relocation camp. At the beginning of World War II, after the Japanese bombed Pearl Harbor, an American naval base in Hawaii, 120,000 Japanese Americans were imprisoned in camps in the United States. Kristi's father spent time in the camps too.

By age six Kristi was ice skating. Her model was Dorothy Hamill, a gold-medal winner in figure skating at the 1976 Winter Olympics. The next year Kristi entered a local skating contest and began taking private lessons. At 12, Kristi joined Rudi Galindo as a pairs partner in competition. They became pairs champions at the Nationals on Long Island, New York, with their "mirror" skating.

Practice took up much of Kristi's day. Her mother woke her at 4 o'clock in the mornings and drove her to 5 o'clock practices at the ice rink. Then at 10 A.M. she went to school. In the evenings there were more practices and study and then an early bedtime so she could start all over again the next day.

In preparation for the Olympics, Kristi finally decided to concentrate on singles skating. Her coach, Christy Kjarsgaard-Ness, had just married and moved to Edmonton, Alberta, Canada. Kristi moved there, too, so she could continue training with Christy. At this time, she had grown to 5 feet tall and weighed 93 pounds.

In the 1991 World Championships in Munich, Germany, she won the gold medal. Two other Americans won, also. This was a first for any country to win all three medals in one contest: Tonya Harding, silver medal; Nancy Kerrigan, bronze medal.

The next big event was the 1992 Olympic Winter Games in the French Alps. The games were held in 650 square miles of mountains around Albertville, France. More than 2,000 athletes from 65 countries entered. Kristi's parents and sister, her coach, and 9,000 spectators watched as she gracefully went through her skating routines to win the Olympic figure skating gold medal.

On her return home, Kristi was given a tremendous welcome. Soon she signed contracts to endorse bottled water, sunglasses, contact lenses, and cream cheese. She even had her picture on cereal boxes and modeled clothing for widely read magazines.

After the Olympic Games, Kristi decided to turn professional and signed a contract to skate for Stars on Ice. Now she appears on television and in ice skating shows around the country.

Reading

1. Kristi spent several hours a day, six days a week practicing figure skating. What does this tell you about her?
2. Make a list of three personal characteristics Kristi possesses. Share your list with a friend. How are the lists the same? different?
3. Draw a picture of Kristi receiving her Olympic gold medal. In a balloon above her, write what you think she was saying.
4. Pretend you are a reporter interviewing Kristi. What three questions will you ask her?

Social Studies

1. Dorothy Hamill was Kristi's model as a child. Do you have a person you want to model after? Share information with your classmates or a friend and tell why you would like to be like him or her.
2. Like Kristi's mother, thousands of Japanese Americans were placed in relocation camps during World War II. In a reference source, read about the camps. Then write a paragraph that gives your opinion of the policy of placing citizens in relocation camps during wartime.
3. In a reference book, read about the European Alps. What makes them the ideal place to hold the Winter Olympics? What are some of the countries that are included in the Alps region?
4. Kristi was very particular about the products she endorsed. If you were in her position, what products would you endorse or not endorse? Why?

Further Reading

Donohue, Shibhan. *Kristi Yamaguchi: Artist on Ice.* Minneapolis, MN: Lerner Publications, 1994.

Gutman, Dan. *Ice Skating: From Axels to Zambonis.* New York: Viking, 1995.

Hilgers, Laura. *Great Skates.* Boston, MA: Little, Brown and Company, 1991.

Kent, Zachary. *U.S. Olympians.* Chicago, IL: Childrens Press, 1992.

The Lincoln Library of Sports Champions. Volume 14. Columbus, OH: Frontier Press Company, 1993.

Lindop, Laurie. *Athletes.* New York: Henry Holt and Company, 1996.

MacLean, Norman. *Ice Skating Basics.* Englewood Cliffs, NJ: Prentice-Hall, 1984.

Ryan, Margaret. *Figure Skating.* New York: Franklin Watts, 1987.

Savage, Jeff. *Kristi Yamaguchi: Pure Gold.* New York: Dillon Press, 1993.

Smith, Pohla. *Superstars of Women's Figure Skating.* Philadelphia: Chelsea House Publishers, 1997.

Yamaguchi, Kristi with Greg Brown. *Always Dream.* Dallas, TX: Taylor Publishing Company, 1998.

Mildred "Babe" Didrikson Zaharias 1911-1956 • Basketball, Track and Field, Golf

One afternoon, Mildred's mother sent her to the grocery store to purchase ground meat for dinner. On the way home she stopped to play baseball for just a moment and laid her package on a bench. Time flew by and Mildred saw her mother running onto the field. "Where's the meat? It's time for supper." There on the bench a hungry dog was devouring the last of it!

Mildred Ella Didrikson gained the nickname "Babe" after baseball slugger Babe Ruth. Baseball was only one of the sports in which Babe excelled. She beat the boys in marbles and won the school tournament in sixth grade. Babe even convinced her neighbors to cut their hedges lower so she could jump them. Later, Babe would say that jumping hedges gave her the practice she needed to jump the hurdles in the track and field meets she entered.

Babe played basketball in high school and her team never lost after she started. Her goal was "to be the greatest athlete that ever lived."

An insurance company offered her a job if she would play on its girls' basketball team. The company sent her to Evanston, Illinois, in 1932 as their one-person track and field team. She won the 80-meter hurdles, the shot-put, the long jump, the javelin throw, and the baseball throw. Babe scored more points than the 23 women on the second-place team. This meet qualified her for the Los Angeles Olympic Games, which were to take place in a few weeks. In the space of 3 hours at the Olympic Games, she won two gold medals and one silver.

Babe was a natural athlete. She was good in bowling, skating, billiards, soccer, and tennis. Although she did not play football, she could pass the ball nearly 50 yards and punt long distances. Once she split the lip of a professional boxing champion as they were sparring. And she even played the harmonica well.

During the 1930s, Babe turned to golf. She practiced till her hands bled, then bandaged them and practiced some more. By the 1940s, she put together a record-breaking winning streak of 17 straight golf tournaments. The Scottish people became very interested in Babe, for golf was the national game in Scotland. Babe participated in the British Women's Amateur Championship golf tournament in 1947.

During practice, Babe chipped a bone in her thumb. She wore a glove over it and told no one. She won the event anyway!

She fell in love with George Zaharias, a wrestler, and they married in 1938. In 1950 the Associated Press named her the Outstanding Woman Athlete of the Half Century. Three years later she had surgery for cancer but battled back in the next year to win five major tournaments. In 1956 the cancer returned, and Babe died.

Reading

1. Why do you suppose Mildred was nicknamed "Babe" by her friends?
2. List from the biography the names of the sports in which Babe played. Read from other references to add more to your list.
3. What incidents in the biography make you believe that athletics were her major interest?
4. Read more about "Babe" Zaharias. Do you think she should rank as "the greatest athlete who ever lived"?

Social Studies

1. What are the three medals given at the Olympic Games?
2. Read about the history of golf in a reference book and take notes so you can tell your class or friends where golf began.
3. Who is your favorite professional golfer—past or present?
4. Find Scotland on a map. If you flew to London, England, what direction would you travel to get to a Scottish golf course?

Further Reading

Anderson, Dave. *The Story of the Olympics.* New York: William Morrow and Company, 1996.

Hahn, James. *Zaharias! The Sports Career of Mildred Zaharias.* Mankato, MN: Crestwood House, 1981.

Kent, Zachary. *U.S. Olympians.* Chicago, IL: Childrens Press, 1992.

Krull, Kathleen. *Lives of the Athletes: Thrills, Spills (and What the Neighbors Thought).* New York: Harcourt Brace & Company, 1997.

The Lincoln Library of Sports Champions. Volume 19. Columbus, OH: Frontier Press Company, 1993.

Lynn, Elizabeth A. *Babe Didrikson Zaharias.* New York: Chelsea House Publishers, 1989.

Osborn, Kevin. *Scholastic Encyclopedia of Sports in the United States*. New York: Scholastic, 1997.

Smith, Beatrice S. *The Babe: Mildred Didrikson Zaharias.* Milwaukee, WI: Raintree Publishers Limited, 1976.

Sullivan, George. *Great Lives: Sports.* New York: Charles Scribner's Sons, 1988.

Wilner, Barry. *Superstars of Women's Golf.* Philadelphia, PA: Chelsea House Publishers, 1997.

Woolum, Janet. *Outstanding Women Athletes: Who They Are and How They Influenced Sports in America.* Phoenix, AZ: The Oryx Press, 1992.

Answer Key

"Hank" Aaron
Social Studies
1. Cooperstown, New York
2. He broke Babe Ruth's career home-run record of 714.
4. South Williamsport, Pennsylvania

Roger Bannister
Social Studies
1. West
2. West; Finnish and Swedish

Bonnie Blair
Social Studies
1. Canada: North America; France and Norway: Europe
3. Ronald Reagan; Jimmy Carter; George Bush
4. My bonnie lies over the sea,
   My bonnie lies over the ocean,
   O bring back my bonnie to me.

Susan Butcher
Social Studies
1. Mt. McKinley
2. Russia
4. Northwest

Roberto Clemente
Social Studies
2. Honduras; Costa Rica; Caribbean Sea; Pacific Ocean
3. Faulting

Nadia Comeneci
Social Studies
3. 1990

Gertrude Ederle
Social Studies
1. Staten Island
2. North Sea and Atlantic Ocean
3. Dover, England, and Calais, France

Chris Evert
Social Studies
2. Collier, Broward, Dade, and Monroe counties; Key West; Everglades National Park

Lou Gehrig
Reading
3. 30; 300

Social Studies
1. Rare, incurable nerve disease; Lou Gehrig's disease
2. Rochester, Minnesota
4. Cal Ripken, Jr.; Baltimore Orioles

Steffi Graf
Reading
3. A serve that one's opponent fails to return and results in a point for the server

Social Studies
1. Neckar and Rhine rivers
2. Australia, France, England, and the United States

Wayne Gretzsky
Social Studies
3. Stanley Cup

Florence Griffith Joyner

Social Studies

1. West
4. 38° north latitude

Sir Edmund Hillary

Reading

2. Sears Tower; Chicago, IL
3. 10,560 feet; 27,545 feet

Social Studies

2. North Island and South Island; North Island
3. 5 miles above sea level
4. Lines of longitude

Michael Jordan

Reading

2. NCAA—National Collegiate Athletic Association; NBA—National Basketball Association

Social Studies

2. Durham; Raleigh

Joan Joyce

Social Studies

1. Chapman University, Orange, California, 1861; Florida Atlantic University, Boca Raton, Florida, 1961

Jean-Claude Killy

Social Studies

2. Paris, flat; Grenoble, mountainous

Olga Korbut

Social Studies

2. Minsk; east

Julie Krone

Social Studies

3. Kentucky Derby—Churchill Downs; Preakness—Pimlico; Belmont Stakes—Belmont Park.

Nancy Lopez

Reading

1. par—number of golf strokes necessary to complete a hole; birdie—a score of one under par on a hole; bogey—a score of one above par on a hole; eagle—a score of two under par on a hole; ace—hitting the golf ball off the tee into the hole in one shot—also called a hole-in-one (Note: Nancy hit four holes-in-one in the same year when she was fifteen!)
2. Sunday; Monday—lunes; Tuesday—martes; Wednesday—miercoles; Thursday—jueves; Friday—viernes; Saturday—sabado; Sunday—domingo

Social Studies

1. Southeast section

Joe Louis

Reading

2. A farmer who gives a share of his crops, rather than rent money, to the person who owns the land.

Alice Marble

Reading

2. singles—two people play; doubles—four people play (generally men against men and women against women); mixed-doubles—a man and woman play on each side.

Social Studies

1. Switzerland was neutral.

Bob Mathias

Reading

2.

Decathlon First Day	Decathlon Second Day
100-Meter Dash	110-Meter Hurdles
Long Jump	Discus Throw
Shot Put	Pole Vault
400-Meter Dash	1,500-Meter Run

Social Studies

2. Denmark; Sweden
3. Sacramento
4. Franklin D. Roosevelt

Martina Navratilova

Social Studies

2. Czech Republic; Slovakia; Prague, Czech Republic
4. Germany, Austria, Slovakia, and Poland

Jesse Owens

Social Studies

1. Lake Erie

"Satchel" Paige

Social Studies

1. Puerto Rico
2. National and American Leagues

Pelé

Social Studies

1. Portuguese
2. Brazil has won the World Cup more times that any other country (three times). The United States has never won the World Cup.

Mary Lou Retton

Social Studies

1. Ohio River; Mississippi River; Gulf of Mexico

Wilma Rudolph

Social Studies

2. Poliomyelitis or infantile paralysis; vaccination

Gale Sayers

Reading

4. Red Grange scored a touchdown the four times he carried the ball against Michigan.

Bill Shoemaker

Reading

3. 1955: Swaps; 1959: Tomy Lee; 1965: Lucky Debonair; 1986: Ferdinand

Social Studies

2. Pacific Ocean

Amos Alonzo Stagg

Social Studies

1. Civil War and Vietnam War

Jim Thorpe

Social Studies

2. Black Hawk

Kristi Yamaguchi

Social Studies

3. Austria, France, northern Italy, Liechtenstein, Slovenia, Switzerland, and southern Germany

"Babe" Didrikson Zaharias

Reading

1. Like baseball player Babe Ruth, she hit many home runs.

Social Studies

1. Gold, silver, bronze
4. North

Index

Index